Correcting Distortions In Your View of God

How to Unload Baggage That Blocks Your Vision

Toni Cooper, Psy. D.

© 2020 Dr. Toni Cooper

All rights reserved.

ISBN: 9781507624005

Unless otherwise indicated, all Scripture is taken from the
New American Standard Bible ®, Copyright © 1960, 1962, 1963,
1968, 1971, 1972, 1973, 1975, 1977, 1995 by The Lockman
Foundation. Used by Permission.

Scripture quotations marked AMP are taken from
THE AMPLIFIED BIBLE, Old Testament © 1965, 1987 by the
Zondervan Corporation. The Amplified New Testament copyright
© 1958, 1987 by the Lockman Foundation. Used by Permission.

Scripture quotations marked TPT are taken from
The Passion Translation®, Copyright © 2017, 2018 by Passion &
Fire Ministries, Inc. Used by permission. All rights reserved.
ThePassionTranslation.com.

I had heard of You
only by the hearing of the ear,
but now my spiritual eye
sees You.

Job 42:5 (AMP)

TABLE OF CONTENTS

Dedication	9
Introduction	10

Part I. Recognizing Distortions

How Fear, Guilt, and Anger Distort	14
Life Experiences and Personal Reality	15
Pit or Palace?	17
Suffering, Trauma, and Distortions	19
The Problem of Suffering	20
Evidence of Distortions	22
Where Does Suffering Come From?	23
Jesus Meets Us in Our Distortions	24
Prayer to Heal From Trauma	26
Perfectionism and Distortions	28
Hidden Perfectionism	29
Toxic Guilt and Shame	31
Distortion: God is Easy to Anger	32
Putting the Pieces Together	35
Prayer to Release Perfectionism	36

Part II. Correcting Distortions

QUIZ: Distortions in Your View of God	40
Jesus Wants Friends Not Slaves	41
People Often Fear Intimacy	42
Word Pictures of God's Loving Attention	43
Cleansing Prayers	44
Prayer For Spiritual Life in Jesus	44
Cleansing From Judgmental Vows	45
The Power of Forgiveness	46
Prayer For a Heart That is Whole	47
Prayer To Release Baggage	48
Prayer To Break Destructive Family Patterns	49

Part III. Faith That Transforms Us

Understanding Body, Soul, and Spirit	53
Experiential Knowledge	54
How Faith Transforms Us	55
The Power of Abiding	56
The Power in Prayer	59
Distortions and Prayer	61
Keys To Spiritual Health and Power	62
God's Word Is Living	62
Personal Devotions	63
Biblical Meditation	65

Keys To Spiritual Health and Power (continued)
    Supernatural Power For Living   68
    In Spirit and In Truth   71
    God's "Miracle Grow" Formula   75
    Biblical Meditation Strategy   78

Spiritual Health and Balance   82
    The Role of Healthy Connections   83
    Protecting Yourself and Your Boundaries   86
        Prayers of Declaration   87
        Understanding Covenant Protection   89

A Lifestyle of Transforming Faith   92
    QUIZ: Transforming Faith   92
    Moving Past Our Comfort Zone   94
    The Thrill of Letting Go   95

Resources and References   97
YouTube Videos   98
Associated Works   99

Dedication

I dedicate this book to the clients, family members, pastors, therapists, and friends who demonstrated the love of God to me. You helped me on my own journey to correct distortions.

INTRODUCTION

"Moses gave us the Law, but Jesus, the Anointed One, unveils truth wrapped in tender mercy." John 1:17 TPT

Many of us are stuck in a view of God that is mostly focused on *our* shortcomings, disappointments, betrayals, failures, and natural abilities. We associate God with churches or authority figures who belittled us. Human logic tells us not to risk too much, expect too much, or dream too big.

Our view of God is often contaminated by human guilt, dysfunctional family, trauma, and condemning doctrines that overly emphasize rules. We call that "baggage".

When the Bible is taught in a way that glorifies rules and minimizes grace, people tend to become proud or discouraged. Many are afraid if we emphasize the love of God that people will get sloppy and fall into sin. We forget that the Bible teaches us that it is the kindness of God that leads a person to repentance (Romans 2:4).

A balanced, accurate view of God will draw us closer to Jesus, build a healthy level of confidence, and increase our resistance to sin. A view of God that emphasizes fear will not ignite our personal passion and certainly does not draw others into faith. It is the love of Jesus that transforms sinners into saints.

I wrote this book to help you recognize and correct deeply held distortions in your image of God. Our personal experiences become baggage or distortions that weigh us down and keep us from enjoying a vital union with the Lord. I want to help you recognize where the distortions come from and take it to the Lord to unload. Then, we can learn Biblical truth with the proper measure of grace.

Before you start each section, you might want to ask the Lord to speak to you. If you have time, look up the verses that are listed in each chapter.

There are questions to help you examine how the reading applies to your life. These are ideas to help you see how the material fits you and can help you clear up some distortions. I also make references to other books and videos that can help you understand an area of faith more deeply. You may want to visit my YouTube channel where you can find short inspirational videos to help you advance in your faith. Many of these videos are listed on page 98 for you.

Let me comment here that I have my own baggage, failures, flaws, and limits. That is part of being human. This book explains my discoveries about how kind and patient God is with us as we navigate life. I apply these principles to my own life and have been privileged to implement them with clients for several decades. I am eager to share these discoveries with others who want to connect with God more deeply.

This book is not a substitute for counseling, medication, or professional help. Please seek immediate attention from a doctor or mental health professional if you are experiencing thoughts of harming yourself or others, triggers from this material, or disruptions in your ability to carry out the tasks of daily living.

I pray that you will receive deeper levels of His love and truth. Then, "with unveiled face" we can all love God, ourselves, and other people with the overflowing joy that God intends for us to have. Jesus voluntarily gave His life so we all can be *free from* guilt and fear and *free to* connect with Him without distortions (2 Corinthians 3:18, John 8:32, I John 4:18).

Toni Cooper, Psy. D.
May 3, 2020

www.drtonicooper.com

Facebook   Dr. Toni Cooper
YouTube   Dr. Toni Cooper
Instagram   tonicooper777

Recognizing Distortions

How Fear, Guilt, and Anger Distort

I became curious about people's view of God after devouring books on inner healing by authors such as David Seamands. I wondered why there are so many people who go to church, are serious about their faith, but live with chronic fear and guilt. I also wondered why, in spite of my faith, I wrestled with bouts of depression and anxiety.

As a psychologist, I noticed that too many people who know the Bible well and even go to church religiously have no peace about being forgiven by God (even when they pray that they are sorry over and over). These sincere believers wonder if God really accepts them or "saved" them. They wonder if God is angry with them.

Many people agonize over not being good enough as a Christian because they believe they are not doing enough. They recognize that their faith is lacking in joy. There are gaps between what they believe ("God is love") and what they feel. Some people actually state they were happier before they started trying to be a good Christian. This shouldn't be!

Since I work a lot with adults who have survived childhood trauma, I also noticed how many people are weighed down with baggage they didn't choose. In spite of effort and faith, many have become passive victims even in their adult lives. The effects of loss, divorce, rejection, abandonment, and/or abuse kept them locked in a view of God (and themselves) that would not move.

So I started studying. I found out that there are many factors that contaminate or distort our view of God. In fact, there is extensive clinical research that examines why people who ascribe to the same religious teachings can have *radically* different experiences of God's love and forgiveness (Rizzuto, 1979).

The following pages summarize decades of personal study and clinical experience counseling adults. I hope this will be a simple yet illuminating journey to help you understand your own hidden distortions that rob you of the joy that has been just beyond your reach. These distortions in our core attitudes and beliefs about God are usually baggage attached to us through early experiences.

Life Experiences and Personal Reality

We each grow up and develop a view of ourselves, other people, the world, and God based on our experiences. A person is shaped most fundamentally by family experiences. (That's why "Family" is the circle closest to the "Person" in my diagram.) We learn to trust, interact, and approach others through family. Family attitudes about love, trust, worth, belonging, the role of authority, and reactions to failure become the core of a human being.

Later, a person goes to school. Relationships outside of the family: school, neighborhood, teams, clubs, church, etc., continue to teach us about our worth, safety in the world, how to belong, and what to expect from peers and authority.

Finally, the climate in our culture (politics, views of men and women, attitudes about my race, advertising and movies, etc.) continues to teach us. We learn where we fit, how to be loved, attitudes toward authority, and what happens when we fail.

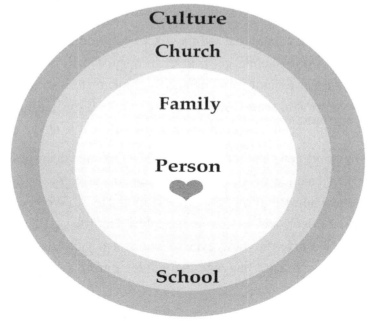

Each of these layers impacts how we view ourselves, other people, life, and what we believe deep down about God. The circles closest to us, from the earliest ages, have the most impact.

By the time children go to school, they already have deeply formed attitudes about whether or not they are lovable, can trust others, can approach authority figures for help, and whether or not the world is safe. ALL of these basic beliefs about life and reality are formed long before we know anything about God. Everything we are taught about God becomes filtered through the grid of these early experiences.

All of these factors color what we think God is like. These experiences impact how we *think* God views us. Some people would rather dismiss God than deal with one more person they think is disappointed with them!

If we mostly had good experiences, then we are likely to have fewer distortions in how we view God and how we believe God views us. So, this is more complex than what kind of church your family attended.

As I stated in the introduction, many of us are stuck in a view of God that is mostly focused on *our* shortcomings, disappointments, betrayals, failures, and natural abilities. We may dismiss God because we expect to be blamed when we fail. Who would love a God like that?

Besides the things that we may have suffered from other people, we may be carrying shame, guilt, or even disgust with ourselves. That unresolved shame or guilt also makes us think that God is mad at us. Again, as we draw near to God, He wants to lift off our guilt and shame so we can lift our heads and enjoy a satisfying life. It is never too late.

The good news is that God is bigger than our distortions. Jesus is the perfect balance of absolute truth and unshakeable love. As we draw close to Him, He allows us to see Him as He is. We become more complete, confident, and loving as we allow His life and truth to flow through us. He gives us new eyes to see as we yield distortions. He shows us how to release baggage that clouds our vision of Him and of ourselves.

Pit or Palace?

Our view of God can mentally put us in a pit or a palace. A harsh view of God will place a person in the basement, or pit, where one feels like a slave. The palace is where we enjoy the love and blessings of God even when our circumstances are unhappy.

Many people have come to understand that, no matter how much their parents loved them, there were times that deep longings weren't met as a child. For people from difficult backgrounds, the pain of hurt and rejection goes even deeper.

If I am carrying guilt, shame, or self rejection then I am less likely to recognize or be comfortable with seeing God as loving. Again, I may have decided, "I'm not lovable so God can't really love me".

The Bible teaches that Jesus suffered and died to make a way for us to be close to God. God invites us to become His friend! Maybe you see why people don't fully respond to God's invitation to approach Him boldly.

We will continue to explore how distortions operate and what you can do to correct them. Now, let's look at the impact of suffering.

Pit Or Palace

- Your view of God as LOVING or eager to Punish

- USUALLY starts with family experiences (how we perceive authority figures)

<u>Questions to Consider</u>

1. What is a new idea to you from this section?

2. Was anything a surprise to you?

3. What are the positive attitudes you got from your early experiences

    about yourself?

    about authority?

    about how to view life?

    about your purpose and value?

4. What are negative things you absorbed from your experiences that may color your view of yourself and how you think God views you?

5. What is hopeful to you from this section?

<u>YouTube Videos</u>:
Dr. Toni Cooper   "Law vs. Grace"
                         "Blessings For Wholeness"
                         "A Prayer For Mending"
A more complete list of videos on my channel is on page 98.

Suffering, Trauma, and Distortions

People have misunderstood Jesus from the beginning. We want and expect God to behave in a certain way. Jesus did NOT arrive on earth or behave the way that people expected. That's why some people did not recognize Jesus as God in human flesh. Jesus was born into poverty, lived in humility, and made His grand entrance into Jerusalem riding a donkey. He allowed Himself to be crucified, dying on a cross, to pay for our personal sin. He showed mercy when the letter of the law would have dictated judgment and death. Instead of judgment, Jesus said "Go and sin no more" to the woman caught in adultery (John 8:1-11).

Even the closest followers of Jesus had problems that distorted their understanding of Him. Look at how the disciples reacted after Jesus was crucified. They were hiding because they were afraid that they would be killed next. Mary ran to tell them when Jesus had risen from the dead. She had seen Jesus with her own eyes but the disciples didn't believe her. Jesus had been telling them all along that He would die and then rise again after three days (Matthew 17:22-23, Luke 9:22, John 2:19).

The disciples didn't receive the good news because they were devastated and terrified. In their grief and faulty understanding about God, they didn't grasp what Jesus had been warning them about. His purpose led to the cross to pay for our sin (Luke 24:46-47, Isaiah 53:1-12). Crucifixion preceded resurrection to bring the kingdom of God to us.

People, then and now, didn't recognize Jesus as God because they had expectations/distortions about how He should act. He didn't judge like they would judge. He didn't take over the government when they wanted heaven to come to earth. Jesus' timing, attitudes, and strategies were not what was expected. He didn't meet people's agendas and expectations.

The Problem of Suffering

When we are suffering or frustrated we may question God. Distortions become evident when God (or life) is disappointing.

We saw in the section on "Personal Reality" that our experiences create the grid for how we understand and interpret life. If our suffering (emotional and physical) as children was met with ridicule or indifference, we will see God as cold and indifferent. If we were punished harshly as children, we are likely to see God as deliberately sending evil to us when bad things are happening. Our early experiences, with parents and authority, color our view of God and our interpretation of suffering (Psalm 77:9-11).

As a psychologist, I talk to many people who believe that God sends tragedy to make us stronger. I think that is a lie of the enemy. It is the devil who comes to kill, steal, and destroy (John 10:10). Jesus came to redeem us and give us abundant life.

Although it is true that God can bring good out of a bad situation, we won't have a joyful confidence in Jesus if we confuse the work of God with the opposition of the devil. Who can love a God who deliberately sends death and illness to make people better? If a human parent tries to protect their child, certainly God is at least as loving as we are!

> "The thief comes only to steal and kill and destroy;
>
> I came that they may have life,
>
> and have it abundantly."
>
> Jesus
>
> John 10:10 NASB

Many people have trouble maintaining a positive view of God when they suffer loss or tragedy. It is even more difficult for a person who has a history of childhood loss, abandonment, adoption, trauma, dysfunction, neglect, or abuse. Many feel abandoned in childhood because of the death of a caretaker, substance abuse issues in the home, divorce, or adoption. These early experiences form our mental grid of what we expect (or dread) for the rest of our lives.

When a child goes through crisis or trauma, they expect a parent to protect them. When a parent is not approachable, is passive, or is an actual source of danger, the expectation develops that no one cares. So, when we don't see answers to prayer as an adult, we can slip back into the grid of seeing God as another angry, unreliable, narcissistic, or aloof authority figure.

EVIDENCE of DISTORTIONS

- Fear
- Response to God Drawing Me
- Consistency and Intensity of Time With God
- Self Condemnation
- Pride
- Response to Others
    - Judgment vs. Seeing Potential
    - Love vs. Take Offense
    - Burden for the lost
- Gaps between beliefs and experience

Once people have been through significant pain, their grid for looking at the world changes. Defensive walls go up around our hearts as protection. (Some of you may remember the song "Doctor My Eyes" by Jackson Browne. He sings about the toll that seeing evil has taken on him. He wonders what it has done to him to resist crying over the things that he has seen.) Walls can make us indifferent. Too much disappointment and we can become negative about ourselves, people, and life in general. It is easy to blame God for the cruelty of life or of people.

The chart above shows places where distortions can operate. Fear, difficulty responding to God, difficulty spending time with God, harsh self condemnation, and stubborn pride are all signs that there are probably some distortions about God and/or some walls around our heart that need attention.

Likewise, when we are quick to judge, easily offended, or cold to the needy, we are probably operating around pain or walls. A significant gap between what we believe in our head about God and what we experience in our hearts also suggests a distortion or wall.

Where Does Suffering Come From?

The problem of suffering has plagued philosophers, theologians, and sensitive souls from ancient times. I don't have a simple answer to clear all of this up for you. I can offer you a perspective based on my own personal suffering, failures, and years of placing my faith in God.

God doesn't send suffering to His children (James 1:17). The Bible teaches that God created a perfect world of harmony and beauty for people to enjoy and cultivate (Genesis 1:26-31). The one rule that God gave to His children was: DON'T eat from the tree of the knowledge of good and evil (Genesis 2:16-17). And, of course, they did. Suffering, disease, loss, and conflict became the norm after that event.

God could have left us in our ruined state. Because of God's love for us, when He implemented the consequences for deliberate rebellion, He also outlined His plan for redemption. God would send a Savior (Jesus Christ) to die for sin and defeat the enemy for us (Genesis 3:15b, Romans 16:20, Galatians 4:4-5). God does not want us destroyed by the tragic things that happen on earth. He is not the author of evil.

Jesus could have stayed in heaven and watched us struggle. Instead, He accepted the assignment of the Father to come to earth (John 1:1-5, 14). He voluntarily paid our debt for sin (Isaiah 53:4-9, Hebrews 12:2).

The rebellion of two people has had extensive consequences for all of us (Romans 5:18-19). However, the Bible also teaches that the death of one person (Jesus Christ), laid down voluntarily for us, has eternal benefits for all of us. We choose our inheritance: the one that comes from rebellion or the one that comes from Jesus. This is the choice that each person makes for themselves.

There are blessings and redemption that come to us when we choose to place our lives back into the hands of Jesus. But as long as we are on earth, there is suffering. Jesus reminds us that "in the world you have tribulation, but take courage; I have overcome the world" (John 16:33).

Jesus Meets Us In Our Distortions

Here is another example of how suffering blinds us from seeing the love of God. The people walking on the road to Emmaus did not recognize Jesus when He came to walk with them after His crucifixion (Luke 24:13-35). They were actually discussing the death of Jesus while He physically walked alongside them. They were talking about how they thought Jesus had come to set them free from Rome but then the leaders had killed Him. They couldn't recognize Jesus right there in front of them because they were lost in their grief. It took time with Jesus explaining the Scriptures to these believers before they finally understood. The Lamb of God had to pay for sin so we could enter the kingdom of God. After they spent time with Jesus their eyes were opened.

Jesus wasn't angry with the men who didn't recognize Him. He joined the travelers as they all walked the road to Emmaus. He took time to explain the plan of God. The plan had not changed. He still loved them. They needed a fresh encounter with God to open their eyes and renew their hope (Ephesians 3:16-19). We will be looking at how to have fresh encounters with God in the pages ahead.

Summary

We looked at a few examples of distortions and how they interfere with people seeing God accurately. Distortions of fear, hurt, abandonment, loss, and grief interfere in our view and enjoyment of God.

We don't think like God thinks (Isaiah 55:8-9). We don't see the big picture. God doesn't send the bad things. However, the bad things can be redeemed and turned around into something good when we place them into God's hands.

In spite of God's love for us, the only place that is totally free of suffering is heaven. So, while we are on earth, we have to wrestle with various kinds of pain (John 16:33). In the meantime, Jesus intercedes for us in heaven (Hebrews 7:25). We also have the Holy Spirit to comfort us and give us power for each day on earth (John 14:16-17).

In Jesus, mercy and truth have kissed (Psalm 85:10, John 1:17). God is the perfect balance of absolute truth and unshakeable love. We will tend to err, as humans, to one side or the other of law or grace. God is love *and* He is holy.

As we see God more clearly, we can receive more of His love and truth with a measure of grace. Then we will more wholeheartedly love God, ourselves, and other people with the overflowing joy that God intended for us to have (Psalm 16:11, Mark 12:29-31, John 17:23). That kind of faith and fire can change us and the world.

This is a prayer you can use to help heal from trauma, loss, and crisis. It incorporates Scripture.

Prayer To HEAL From Trauma

Lord, I want to be free from the past. I want to move on with my life and be free from hurt, anger, and pain.

I CHOOSE to forgive _____ for what they did to me. I release them to YOU to handle them. I ask You for wisdom about this person.

I ask YOU to TAKE the anger, hurt, and fear that I carry into YOUR body on the Cross where you paid for my sin and the sin committed against me.

I ask You, Lord, to SOOTHE the areas of my brain that keep me on high alert. Please BALANCE my thinking with my emotions as You intended for me. Please restore my sense of SAFETY.

Please forgive me for my sins. Please fill my heart with Your life, Jesus.

I ask You to strengthen me at the core of my being. Fill me with Your resurrection power so I can be fully alive: body, soul, and spirit. Amen.

Isaiah 53:5   2 Timothy 1:7   Ephesians 3:16   Colossians 2:10

Questions to Consider

1. What is a new idea to you from this section?

2. What personal experiences have negatively colored your

    view of yourself?

    view of other people?

    expectations of God?

3. What do you think may be a source of distortion for you?

4. What is your reaction to James 1:17 that God sends good gifts to His children?

5. What is hopeful to you from this section?

Resources:

YouTube videos "A Prayer to Heal from Trauma", "Restoring Identity, Dignity, and Destiny", and "Are You Trapped In A Vow?" by Dr. Toni Cooper. A list of videos is on page 98.

A Bible study that examines the goodness of God, personal suffering, and growing through prayer and worship is Breaking Through To Blessing (listed on page 99).

Perfectionism and Distortions

Many people have perfectionistic tendencies and expectations that they don't recognize. If you have those tendencies, or if you grew up with an authority figure who was a perfectionist, then those tendencies are likely to fuel some distortions in your view of God.

A critical parent (or coach or family member) often creates a situation where we try to be perfect to avoid criticism. Also, first born children can become little adults who strive for perfection because they are trying to be like the adults in the home. Anyone who grows up too fast due to loss, sickness, addiction, or trauma is also likely to have perfectionist tendencies. (That sounds like almost everyone, doesn't it?)

Add to that, a home where there is favoritism or a lot of competition (between the kids or between parent and child) can create perfectionism and unrealistic expectations. Individuals in this kind of environment need to prove themselves over and over to get attention or validation. There is a sense that they are never good enough. Sometimes they can't just sit still and relax because *that* is "lazy". They may become workaholics, overly driven to achieve, or unduly focused on pleasing others in order to prove their worth.

It is easy to see how this contaminates our view of God. If *we* are hard on ourselves, we will assume God looks at us the same way. If we grew up with someone who was too hard on us, then we are likely to assume God looks at us harshly.

You can see that these experiences of criticism, rejection, undue competition, disappointment, or high expectations negatively impact our view of ourselves. These expectations and undercurrents impact

- How WE think God views us.
- How we THINK God judges us.

It is necessary to forgive ourselves and others for the imbalances that stir up all this confusion. Suggested prayers to help you release forgiveness are peppered throughout the next few sections.

Hidden Perfectionism

You can think of perfectionism as needing to be perfect, but it shows up in many forms. Similar to perfectionism is:

- Self criticism where I am never happy with my looks, performance, status, or behavior. I constantly compare myself with others.

- Expectations that I can handle everything well, without help, in spite of how I am feeling or how many things are happening.

- Demands I place on myself to do more, be more efficient, and try harder.

This translates spiritually into what David Seamands calls "striving". It is the idea that if I try hard enough, God will be happy with me (or I won't hate myself). The Bible teaches that we are loved and valued by God apart from our efforts. We cannot earn our way to salvation or to MORE of God's love. Our connection is secure through our faith in Christ's payment for our sin (Ephesians 2:8-9, Romans 4:3-5, John 10:9-11).

This unconditional love, initiated by God towards us, is hard for many people to accept. Most people seem to have the mental grid that love must be earned by achievement, charm, status, success, or some other effort. Most of us are not comfortable with being loved just for being ourselves. And yet, that *is* what many people long for at their core.

If you think about it, the religious people in the Bible who were big on rules and short on love and compassion were the Pharisees. They attacked and argued with Jesus. Jesus confronted them about their pride and spiritual blindness. When our faith is driven by the need to earn God's approval, we have lost our bearings (Galatians 4:7, 9; Galatians 5:4-5).

You can see how it is easy to get stuck in a view of God that is based on OUR performance instead of HIS payment. It is hard to maintain joy or peace if we are approaching God with an attitude of perfectionism or striving.

And you did not receive
the spirit of religious duty,
leading you back
into the fear
of never being good enough.

But you have received
the Spirit
full of acceptance,
enfolding you
into the family of God.

Romans 8:15a TPT

Toxic Guilt and Shame

Experts distinguish guilt from shame. Guilt says I feel bad because of *what I've done*. Shame says *I* am bad. Guilt is normal when we've done something bad. It helps people be civilized. Guilt is resolved by apologizing and making things right with other people or with God (I John 1:9). Shame is probably never healthy.

A person who grows up with lots of criticism, shaming, or guilt for normal mistakes is more likely to have trouble with self acceptance. Some then rebel completely against God, are drawn to religious groups that are excessively strict and authoritarian (like cults, for example), or have trouble accepting forgiveness. Toxic guilt or shame is perpetuated by churches who are heavy on rules and duty (religion) and light on extending grace. Only Jesus has the perfect balance of mercy and truth.

Chronic guilt and shame are born out of a sense of rejection. One grows up with the feeling, from family or harsh religion, that they are always wrong or bad. This attitude is tied into a distortion of God as very easy to anger. It is born out of harsh authoritarian experiences.

Much has been written on the way that we subconsciously associate the shortcomings of parents or authority figures with the way that we view God. If my parents held grudges or gave me the silent treatment when I misbehaved, then I will have trouble recognizing that God is quick to forgive me. If I was rejected by parents, siblings, or peers, then I may come to feel unworthy of love. I then resist receiving love if I have already concluded that I don't deserve to be loved.

Religion	vs. GRACE
Striving	Acceptance
Fear	Peace
Weariness	Rest
Formula	Freedom
Rules & Duty	Creativity
Tradition	Relationship
Guilt	Forgiveness

Distortion: God Is Easy To Anger

You can see that people have many distortions or blind spots in the way that they view God. None of us sees Him completely clearly, of course, until we reach heaven (I Corinthians 13:9-13). However, the more the distortions operate the less we experience the love, power, forgiveness, and acceptance that God provides for us.

Previously I mentioned that another very common distortion is the view that God is very demanding and quick to get angry. You might already be able to figure out how a person would develop that view of God.

One place Jesus addressed this misconception is when He said "My yoke is easy and My burden is light" in Matthew 11:30. Jesus taught in word pictures to help us shift our view of God (and correct our distortions). Here are some of the pictures Jesus gives us of God's care:

- A shepherd and the sheep (John 10:1-18).
- A mother hen and her young (Luke 13:34).
- Friendship (John 15:12-17).
- A tree and its branches in a vineyard (John 15:1-11).

Each of these pictures demonstrates the protection, provision, and/or committed bond that God offers His followers. Sheep, chickens, friends, or branches *do not earn* their place. The Shepherd cares for the sheep at the sacrifice of His own life. (That is exactly what our salvation cost Jesus.) The mother hen gathers her young and keeps them under her protective watch. A friend shares secrets and plans (John 15:15, Psalm 25:14). A tree provides the nurture for each branch. Jesus wants us to see that He is the initiator and the source for our relationship.

Sheep, chicken, or friends can run away from the protective care and limits. But their efforts did not earn them the relationship. It is hard for us to grasp the truth that we do not earn our place with God from day to day.

Let's consider the example of the tree and branch from John 15 more closely. A branch draws its life from the vital union with the tree. On its own, the branch has no life. (Jesus is primarily teaching about spiritual life here.) The branch does not *earn* its connection to the tree. It just lives in union with the tree that provides *all* the nutrition.

I think Jesus was trying to tell us that supernatural life, power, love, and faith come from staying close to Him (the "true vine"). This union with Jesus is eternal life, protection, companionship, and supernatural power for lasting fruit in our lives. That's why He said "apart from Me you can do nothing" (John 15: 5b). Supernatural power comes from the outflow of our union with Jesus - not from religious effort.

Instead of us performing to earn God's love and please Him, He wants to fill us with Himself. His life, overflowing in us through the Holy Spirit, gives us love and goodness we do not have in our own strength. Life comes from Him at every step of the walk of faith.

A life of faith is not a set of rules. (Although when we experience the love of God, we will want to stay close to Him rather than indulge in harmful, forbidden practices that lead to trouble.) It is the goodness of God that leads us to repentance in our daily attitudes and choices (Romans 2:4). A relationship with Jesus means I lean into Him each day for the flow of my life. This type of life is not rooted in fear of an angry, judgmental god. Love and connection is the foundation of this union from start to finish.

When we live under the distortion that God is easily angered or that we have to constantly work to please God, we will wear ourselves out. We are more likely to be critical of ourselves and others when we live under the law instead of a secure confidence in the love and grace of Jesus Christ. God is love (I John 4:16). Mercy and truth are united perfectly in Jesus (John 1:14-17). God has provided the Lamb for our cleansed union with Him (John 1:29, John 1:36, John 3:16). We abide in Him each day to enjoy the benefits of that union.

To know you is to experience

a flowing fountain,

drinking in your life,

springing up to satisfy.

In your light we receive the light of revelation.

Psalm 36:9   TPT

Putting the Pieces Together

By now you can see that the factors that influence our view of God are complex and layer over time. But that is not a problem. We have outlined some of the ways that distortions are formed. Let's summarize and then make more corrections.

1. People are afraid of God (and sometimes angry with Him) due to early experiences of criticism, rejection, abuse, loss, or abandonment.
2. People feel ashamed of their own failures and often don't know how to deal with them.
3. It is normal to have distortions about God. Even the disciples who spent three years with Jesus could not grasp what He was saying until He died on the cross and then rose from the dead.
4. Jesus suffered and died to make a way for us to be close to God. God invites us to be His friend.
5. Considering that God went to all this trouble to draw us closer, we may wonder why we don't respond more readily to His loving invitations. He longs to forgive us, cleanse us, and empower us to live an extraordinary life.

We have looked at layers of personal reactions, motivation, and attitudes. Mostly, we have looked at reactions of fear and guilt. These internal pressures and assumptions can also fuel chronic irritability or depression in some people. If you want to read more on these topics, and the role of grace, I recommend the book <u>Healing For Damaged Emotions</u>.

Regardless of how various internal pressures and assumptions play out in an individual, the spiritual corrections are very similar. In the next section we will look more closely at the ways God invites us into a place of joy, peace, and power.

Here is a prayer you can use if you would like to address some of these concepts with God yourself. The following prayer may help you soften perfectionistic tendencies.

Prayer To Release Perfectionism

I choose to forgive _____ for the criticism, demands, and lack of approval that led me to develop perfectionism and excessive demands on myself and others.

I admit my sin of resentment or anger I have carried against _____ because of the pressure they put on me.

I repent for any unhealthy pride I have taken in being a perfectionist. I repent for any ways I have placed harsh, unrealistic expectations on others.

I ask You, Lord, to take the shame, fear, anger, and any sense of rejection I have carried into YOUR body on the cross. I ask You to forgive all my sin and help me to walk in a balance of love, truth, and excellence without striving for perfectionism.

I accept Your forgiveness for my sins and mistakes. Only You are perfect, Lord Jesus. I choose to forgive myself. Thank you that You love me and accept me. I yield myself to You, Lord Jesus.

Questions to Consider

1. What is a new idea to you from this section?

2. Where do you see tendencies towards perfectionism in yourself?

3. Where do you see tendencies to work for God instead of leaning into Jesus each day?

4. What is your reaction to Romans 8:15 that God accepts you?

5. What is helpful to you from this section?

Resources:

John Arnott   The Importance of Forgiveness
David Seamands   Healing For Damaged Emotions

YouTube Videos:
Dr. Toni Cooper   "Reducing Perfectionism"
                       "How To Ask God For Forgiveness"
                       "How To Finally Forgive"
                       "Toxic Guilt and Shame"

Correcting Distortions

Quiz on Distortions

Here are some TRUE or FALSE statements. How do you see God?

_____ 1. It is important that I work hard to please God.

_____ 2. God is easily disappointed in me.

_____ 3. I can count on my church/pastor/priest to explain God to me.

_____ 4. Praying in my car or listening to messages on the radio are great ways to stay connected to God.

_____ 5. I should keep telling God how sorry I am for a sin.

_____ 6. Suffering and tragedy are things God sends to make me stronger.

_____ 7. When I feel tormented about a sin, that is from God.

_____ 8. Since God will forgive me later, it is okay if I do things now that I know are wrong.

Here is what the Bible says about these opinions. You can look up the verses if you like. (All of the statements above are false according to the Bible.)

1. Matthew 11:28   Ephesians 2:8-9   Psalm 46:10

2. Romans 8:1   Psalm 103:8, 13, 14 Isaiah 1:18

3. I Timothy 2:5   Acts 17:11   Mark 7:13

4. Psalm 46:10   John 17:17   Isaiah 30:15

5. I John 1:9   Romans 8:1   Psalm 103:11-12

6. James 1:17   Matthew 6:13   John 10:10

7. I John 1:9   Romans 8:1   Psalm 85:8a

8. Galatians 6:7   John 14:23   Hebrews 3:13

Jesus Wants Friends Not Slaves

I thought it might be helpful to look again at how God describes Himself in the Bible. He introduces and explains Himself to us in various ways through the Old and New Testaments. Let's examine how God wants us to see Him.

When I first came to know the Lord as my Savior, I was fascinated by Psalm 23 and the verses that portrayed Jesus as a shepherd. I had been raised in a church where God seemed angry, demanding, and eager to send people to hell. There were lots of rules and I did try to follow them. But I never felt connected to God.

> I am the Good Shepherd who
>
> lays down my life as a sacrifice for the sheep.
>
> Jesus
>
> John 10:11   TPT

After I was introduced to the idea that I could have a personal connection to God, because Jesus paid for my sin, I really started looking at what Jesus said about Himself. I wanted to see what it means to have a relationship with Him that was a real connection.

Earlier, we saw how Jesus compares Himself to a shepherd. A shepherd cares for the sheep. He protects them from wolves. He knows each one individually and sees what they need at the end of each day. A good shepherd will put himself in harm's way to save the sheep. He speaks to them, sings to them, and leads them to peaceful places to rest. This God is committed to my wellbeing! (If this view of Jesus intrigues you like it does me, I would encourage you to read <u>A Shepherd Looks at Psalm 23</u>.)

Unlike "friending" or "following" a person on social media (whom you may barely know), Jesus is looking for people with whom He can share His thoughts and secrets. Jesus wants us to be His friends, not His slaves (John 15:15, Romans 8:15).

We're not accustomed to thinking of God as friendly. We looked at how many see God as distant, angry, and/or hard to please. We think this way in spite of the fact that God invites us to approach Him with boldness.

Hebrews 4:16 Therefore let us draw near with confidence to the throne of grace, so that we may receive mercy and find grace to help in time of need.

Psalm 25:14 The secret of the LORD is for those who fear Him, And He will make them know His covenant.

People Often Fear Intimacy

Many people in this day and age are fearful of intimacy with people, much less deep connection with God. They grew up in homes where people were detached or smothering. Perhaps this is another reason why God gives us a variety of pictures of Himself in the Bible. We need His help so we can understand how *safe* and *loving* He is even though He is a mighty God! He wants to meet every kind of need at our deepest level so we can be in a rich, vital union with Him.

> **I love each of you with the same love that the Father loves me.**
>
> **You must continually let my love nourish your hearts.**
>
> Jesus
>
> John 15:9 TPT

Word Pictures of God's Loving Attention

Father	Matthew 6:9	Malachi 3:17	Psalm 103:13
	Isaiah 63:16	Isaiah 64:8	Isaiah 43:6-7
Mother	Isaiah 49:15	Isaiah 66:13	Luke 13:34
Spouse	Isaiah 54:4-6	Isaiah 62:2-5	Jeremiah 31:32
	Hosea 2:19-20		
Brother	Matthew 12:50		
Friend	John 15:13-15	Proverbs 18:24	

Our broken lenses of bad experience make it hard to receive this love and care from God sometimes. Many are afraid, on some level, that He will overwhelm us, judge us, and try to control us. God wants us to know on an *experiential* level how available, strong, and gentle He is to His children.

I find it helpful to remember that Jesus is pictured as The Lamb of God because He paid for sin (John 1:29, 1:36) and The Lion of Judah because He is the King who opposes evil (Revelation 5:5). When I need His gentleness, He is the Lamb of God for me. When I need strength to fight a battle, He is the Lion who helps me stay in the fight. (You can also see this depiction of God's strength, goodness, and gentleness in the Narnia series that begins with <u>The Lion, The Witch, and the Wardrobe</u>.)

The type of relationship that God invites us into is healing and transformational. This type of connection goes beyond the information level of what we believe in a religious sense. We could never earn that kind of connection to God.

Cleansing Prayers

On the next few pages are some prayers you can use to help position yourself in a solid relationship with Jesus. There are also prayers to help you release yourself from various distortions. Every step you take spiritually can help clean up distortions.

Prayer For Spiritual Life in Jesus

If we want God's supernatural power for life, then it is important to follow God's prescription for proper alignment of spirit, soul, and body. Jesus said:

> "I am the Way,
>
> I am the Truth,
>
> and I am the life.
>
> No one comes next to the Father
>
> except through union with me."
>
> John 14:6 TPT

Lord Jesus,

I acknowledge that You are God who voluntarily died to pay for my sin (John 10:18). You had no sin but You paid for all of mine. I want to be clean and free from sin. I ask You to be my Savior. I yield my life to You from now on. Fill my heart and mind with Your truth. Teach me how to live in a healthy way that pleases You. Thank You for Your gift of salvation to me. Amen.

Cleansing From Judgmental Vows

John 11:44 TPT   Lazarus...still had grave clothes tightly wrapped around his hands and feet and covering his face! Jesus said to them, "Unwrap him and let him loose."

Like Lazarus, we are raised to new life when we respond to the call of Jesus. Like Lazarus, there are coverings over our eyes that need to be removed. Then we can walk out of the darkness and into our future with clear vision.

You can use this prayer to cleanse yourself from assumptions or vows you may have made (consciously or subconsciously) that cloud your vision and the path of life. (You might want to say this prayer out loud.) Many times people slip into these attitudes early in life. Often, people don't recognize these vows are limiting the freedom of their hearts and minds.

In the NAME of JESUS I come out of agreement with the LIES that:

    I am not good enough.

    I am not worthy of love.

    I do not belong.

In the NAME of JESUS I renounce any VOWS I might have made that:

    I will not trust.

    I will not feel.

    I will never allow myself to be hurt again.

Thank You, Lord, that You set me free from wrong beliefs and harmful vows.

Help me, from now on, to fill my heart and mind with Your truth. Amen.

The Power of Forgiveness

Jesus wants you free from the effects of hurt, criticism, and rejection. In fact, He died to pay for our sin *and* the sin committed against us. Those memories and injuries tie us to the past. Unfortunately, resentment and unforgiveness also tie us to people and the past. Those unresolved experiences are blinders that distort our vision for ourselves and our future. They are "baggage". Prolonged resentment harms our emotional wellbeing, physical health, and relationships (Hebrews 12:15). That's why, I believe, we are told to forgive others (Matthew 6:12, Luke 6:37). Forgiveness helps remove our distortions, toxins, and baggage.

Before you get mad and skip the rest of the reading, please chew on this next paragraph. Forgiving *doesn't* mean that what they did is okay. It doesn't mean you should trust them. But, we can't wait for the feeling to forgive because *that feeling probably isn't coming*! When we CHOOSE to forgive (not just ask for the strength to forgive) then we allow God to remove the "dirt" from our spiritual vision. Then, we are free to encounter God (and people) with less baggage (Hebrews 12:15). It also improves our emotional and physical health.

The next few prayers incorporate forgiveness to help eliminate some sources of pain, distortion, and baggage. Then our view of ourselves, safe people, and God becomes clearer. The freedom and restoration of your peace of mind is worth the pain of choosing to forgive. Jesus voluntarily died so we can enjoy freedom and restoration.

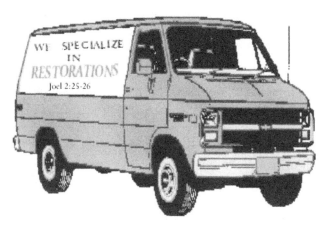

Prayer For a Heart That is Whole

I ask You, Lord, to break any deep, hidden connections I have made between You and harsh authority figures, parents, spouses, or people who have expected too much and given back too little to me. (Name those people the Lord shows you.) I choose to forgive them as an act of my will.

Lord, You are NOT a flawed human being that you would lie to me, use me, neglect me, or get tired of me. You love me more than I love myself. I repent for the things I have projected onto You that began with other people or within myself.

I ask You to fill every dark, empty, or wounded place in my soul with Your love that casts out fear, Your peace that calms me, the faith that You want good things for me, discernment to love wisely, and the promise that in You my latter days will be greater than the former. Show me what to let go of and what to pursue. Give me a heart of wisdom!

Please knit me back together as You intended me to be: whole in body, soul, and spirit. Please enable me to love You, myself, and others with a whole heart. I ask you to free my heart, mind, and body to be fully alive.

I ask You for a heart that is healed by Your love and filled with Your Spirit. Thank You for Your love and kindness to me that is fresh every morning.

Show me, Lord, anything else You want me to know or see today. Baptize me again in Your love! Thank You, Lord, that it is Your will that I see You as You truly are.

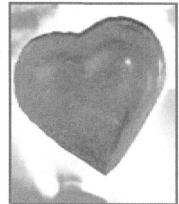

Prayer To Release Baggage

Lord, I *choose* to forgive those who have injured me financially, emotionally, sexually, physically, or spiritually. I make the choice to forgive _____ (insert as many names as needed).

I release them *from* my judgment and release them *to* You.

I repent for any resentments I have harbored against them, knowingly or unknowingly. I ask you to carry away the effects of these sins committed against me or by me. I repent for agreeing with their judgments against me.

I release to You any pain that I carry in my heart, mind, or body. I give You permission to take any anger, hurt, shame, fear, pride, resentment, self pity, or guilt that I have carried. I release to You the emotions that I have hidden so I can look strong or tough. I release those toxic emotions into Your body on the cross where all this was paid for.

I come out of agreement with any *vows* I have made not to feel, not to trust, or not to hope. I renounce any false beliefs I have accepted from others about myself. I renounce the lie that I am _____ taken on from loss, criticism, rejection, or pain. (Fill in any negative, self-critical attitudes you have come to believe about yourself in that space.)

In the name of Jesus, I ask You to break all entanglements and unhealthy ties that remain between me and the individuals who caused me harm. I ask You to break any unhealthy bonds to loss, trauma, or rejection. I ask You to break any unhealthy ties to organizations or places. Help me fill my heart and mind with Your truth about myself and life.

Thank You, Lord Jesus, that I am set free in You.

Prayer To Break Destructive Family Patterns

Lord, You created family and intended them to be a source of joy and safety. Through the generations, Your plan has been corrupted and families pass down bad things as well as the good You intended.

I pray this prayer, Lord, to cleanse anything I have done or inherited through my family line. I want my children and myself to be free from destructive patterns.

I repent on behalf of my family line, on both sides, as far back as You can see, Lord. I repent for breaking commandments where we did not put You first, used Your name as a curse, worshipped false gods, failed to honor the Sabbath, rebelled against parents, caused violence, lied, stole, or committed sexual sin. I repent for myself and on behalf of my family for secret sins, secret vows, and occult practices that You call an "abomination" in Your word.

I renounce those practices, sins, and the addictions in my life and in my family line. I ask for You to apply the shed blood of Jesus (Exodus 12:21-24, Isaiah 53:4-12) to cover those sins. I thank You for dying on the cross, voluntarily, so that we have Your resurrection power to break these patterns that have passed from generation to generation.

I worship You as the only true God. I ask You to continue to draw each of us closer to You, Lord Jesus. I ask You to fill our eyes with Your light (Psalm 36:9, Ephesians 1:18) and draw each of us to Your path of life (Psalm 16:11). Thank You, Jesus, that You are releasing all the blessings that You originally designed for our family. Amen.

<u>References:</u>
Ten Commandments   Exodus 20:1-17
Forbidden Spiritual Practices   Deuteronomy 18:10-14
    Leviticus 19:31   Leviticus 20: 6, 27

(You can be forgiven for these practices if you renounce them. You can see that the Bible warns us seriously about spiritual activities that are false worship.)

Questions to Consider

1. What is a new idea to you from this section?

2. Is there anything you aren't ready to pray about?

3. Below is a paraphrase of Isaiah 30:15 I have written. If you like, you can pray this over yourself as a blessing. You can try placing your name into the verse. I capitalized some of the words to emphasize and draw out the meaning of the verse.

> For thus the LORD GOD, the HOLY ONE of Israel, has said:
> In withdrawing from YOUR unholy alliances
> > and making yourself at home in ME,
> > > ceasing from your OWN efforts,
>
> I will release MY sufficiency, deliverance from distress,
> > and FREEDOM to move FORWARD.
>
> As you cease from your activity, RESTING confidently
> > in My loving, faithful character
>
> you will be SECURE and tranquil - without worry -
> > regardless of what is happening around you.
>
> And you WILL assert ROYAL privilege, POWER,
> > and VITALITY in your battles because of Me.

YouTube Videos: "Life Without Baggage"   "Blessings For Wholeness"

Faith That Transforms Us

And on this mountain

He will swallow up the covering

which is over all peoples,

Even the veil which is stretched over all nations.

… And the Lord GOD will wipe tears away from all faces.

Isaiah 25: 7, 8b

NASB

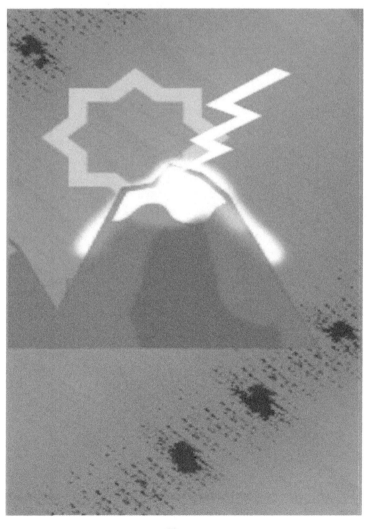

Understanding Body, Soul, and Spirit

We are designed by God as spirit, soul, and body (I Thessalonians 5:23). Each of these dimensions of our being needs attention and each of these impact the other.

Counseling helps people change by talking about the issues of the soul. Counseling is effective, but there are some situations where wounds to the soul (heart, emotions, thoughts, attitudes, etc.) are very slow and painful to resolve. Medicine helps make corrections to imbalances in the body. (There is much research that indicates a healthy spiritual life benefits the body and emotions.) The remainder of this book looks at spiritual strategies to correct distortions.

If you are struggling with any serious problems, or are not getting relief for your concerns from a spiritual approach, then it may be time to meet with an expert in treating the soul (counselor, psychologist, or social worker) or the body (family doctor, nurse practitioner, internist, neurologist, or psychiatrist). Any thoughts of harming yourself or others deserves *immediate* attention from your doctor.

The next sections give you insights and strategies for how to build your spirit through a healthy faith. These spiritual practices have helped people through the ages develop deep and powerful spiritual lives. Once you have established your relationship with Jesus, you choose (not earn) how much you are going to allow your spirit to grow. As you grow and mature in your faith, your spiritual power increases, you allow God to remove layers of distortions, and you begin to impact others with the life of Jesus that you carry.

We can begin this process of empowering your spirit by revisiting the idea of experiential knowledge of God. Our connection to God can be deeper than what we believe intellectually.

> Taste and see that the Lord is good;
>
> Psalm 34:8a

Experiential Knowledge

One of the distinctions of the Christian faith is that it is not just a set of beliefs. It is a relationship (John 1:12, Romans 8:15). Certainly, there are teachings in the Bible that are taught as absolutes (Matthew 5:17, Romans 3:31). However, the Christian life starts with a relationship with Jesus. This relationship with God is free because of the payment Jesus made for our sin.

There are many people who believe in God, who may even go to church, but they do not have a vibrant connection to God. The Bible tells us that even the devil knows who God is and trembles (James 2:19). The Pharisees could quote the Bible but they were the ones who plotted the death of Jesus. So intellectual knowledge and correct doctrine are not the same as spiritual life.

Adam and Eve "knew" each other in the Garden (Genesis 4:1). Mary, the mother of Jesus, was confused how she could become pregnant, since she had not "known" a man (Luke 1:34). Those two passages describe the experiential knowledge that occurs in a sexual union. The concept of knowing someone in a deep, personal (but nonsexual) way goes beyond how we usually think about knowing God.

The Song of Solomon is a whole book devoted to the illustration that God dotes on His Bride (us) who is preoccupied with her True Love (Him). Jesus challenged His followers to eat His flesh and drink His blood (which drove many away according to John 6:66). So God calls us into an encounter with Him that goes beyond our brain power and touches us at the core.

How Faith Transforms Us

Once we have a real relationship with Jesus, we can begin to cultivate that connection. Jesus calls us deeper. As in any relationship, the time we devote to that connection will determine the depth and the quality of that relationship.

We define the depth and quality of our connection depending on our response to God. It takes time and effort to get to know another person. So it is in *knowing* God. This is not performance and His love is not earned. But connection is cultivated.

Transformational, healthy faith is not based on rules or duty. A vibrant faith is overflowing with what the Bible calls the "fruit" of the Holy Spirit. This overflow of God's character into our personality is described in Galatians 5:22.

> But the fruit produced by
> the Holy Spirit within you
> is divine love in all its varied expressions:
> joy that overflows,
> peace that subdues,
> patience that endures,
> kindness in action,
> a life full of virtue,
> faith that prevails,
> gentleness of heart, and
> strength of spirit.
> Never set the law above these qualities,
> for they are meant to be limitless.
>
> Galatians 5:22-23 TPT

> But we all,
>
> with unveiled face, beholding as in a mirror
>
> the glory of the Lord,
>
> are being transformed into
>
> the same image
>
> from glory to glory...
>
> 2 Corinthians 3:18 NASB

The Power Of Abiding

Positive transformation of the soul (mind, will, and emotions) is a process (Phil. 1:6). The more that we intentionally worship, pray, and practice the presence of God, the more we participate with God in that process (which the Bible calls sanctification). Taking time to rest in the presence of God allows God to give us peace, shift our perspective, strengthen our core, and make us fully alive (Colossians 2:10).

God pursues us. We respond when we rest in His presence, stop to read His word and encounter Him, talk with Him, wait for His leading, sing to Him, or quietly enjoy His sweetness. We enter His glory and we are changed to become our best.

We can respond to His invitation to "Come up higher" (Rev 4:1) in these simple ways and enter a realm we cannot see with our eyes. Our spirits are fed and nurtured. We find rest for our souls in His gentle presence. Our hunger for more of God increases. He gently corrects our distortions as we feed on His word.

Time we spend being mindful of the presence of God changes us. Normal people can have life changing encounters with God when we seek Him. Being mindful of God's presence has been called "the practice of the presence of God" by a man named Brother Lawrence.

Brother Lawrence's writings in the 1600's became a book called The Practice of the Presence of God. He determined to live in a state of abiding (John 15) where, no matter what he was doing, he reminded himself throughout the day that the Lord was there with him. It changed his life and impacted other people.

Now, obviously, we are always in God's presence (even if we don't believe in Him). He is everywhere and He knows everything. God is ever mindful of us. As we become mindful of His quiet companionship, we find comfort. This is also a form of worship (Psalm 46:10-11, Psalm 23:1-3).

A more earthly version of this principle of practicing God's presence is romantic infatuation. I often remind people of how they acted when they fell in love. When that happens, you become preoccupied with the object of your affection regardless of what you are doing. They are always present somewhere in your thinking. There is an eager anticipation of the next encounter. (Perhaps that is one reason why the Lord describes Himself as a bridegroom in parts of Scripture.) The depth of that special connection dominates everything that goes on day to day.

David spent years of his life as a shepherd worshipping God and writing the Psalms. He was not perfect. In fact, he had many failures. But the Bible calls David "a man after God's own heart" (I Samuel 13:14). He didn't seek information *about* God. He sought God Himself. And we are told that those who seek Him with their whole heart will find Him (Jeremiah 29:13).

So, time reading the Bible can be work like reading a textbook. Or, it can be an encounter with the One who loves me and thinks about me all day long. I can listen to the Lord as I read and talk to Him. The one approach is intellectual and stale. The other is a spiritual infusion that quickens and empowers me.

I am changed in His presence by His living word (Hebrews 4:12). That is the difference between rules and grace. Take time to cultivate your spiritual life with God. He will take you from glory to glory (2 Corinthians 3:18). He gently corrects your distortions.

Questions to Consider

1. What is a new idea to you about God?

2. What is the difference between spirit, soul, and body?

3. What is the importance of nurturing your spiritual connection to God?

4. What is the difference between making a commitment to Jesus for salvation and growing spiritually?

YouTube Videos:
Dr. Toni Cooper   "Harnessing The Power Of The Spirit"
                           "Strengthening Your Spirit"
                           "Aglow With The Spirit"
                           "How To Read The Bible and Understand It"

> Be *still*
>
> And know that I am God.
>
> Psalm 46:10

The Power in Prayer

A conversation involves talking and listening. I think of reading the Bible as listening to what God is saying (although we can talk and interact with Him while reading the Bible). Prayer is really talking to God and you can use your own words.

In any relationship, the level of openness and communication is a good indicator of the depth of that relationship. So it is with God. If our prayer occurs ONLY while multitasking, it is probably going to stay shallow. However, if we are still, we may sense a new thought or insight while we are praying. Oftentimes, but not always, that impression comes from God for us. (I can often tell when an insight comes from God because it is always a much better idea than I could have created.)

If you are new to prayer, just set aside a few minutes to pray after you have spent some time in the Bible. Since you are learning to abide in the presence of God during the day, you can certainly "shoot up" a quick prayer to interact with God any time during your day. But there will be more quality in your prayer time if at least part of it is quietly focused on God (rather than multitasking). You can pray while you are kneeling, walking, standing, sitting, etc. The position of your heart is more important than the position of your body.

If you are more practiced in prayer, there are suggestions on the next page on how to increase the power and effectiveness of your prayers. These are suggestions not rules. Again, the important thing is that God wants us to approach Him and talk to Him. He *looks for* people who turn to Him in spirit and in truth (John 4:23-24).

How To Have POWER In Your Prayers

Seek Me and *you will find Me.* Jeremiah 29:13

1. Use <u>Scripture</u>. God's word has power!
   Isaiah 55:10-11   Hebrews 4:12   2 Timothy 3:16

2. Ask God to <u>cleanse</u> you before you pray.   I John 1:9

3. Pray in <u>Jesus'</u> name. Jesus paid for our sins and He is the one who gives us access to the Father.
   Hebrews 4:15-16   I Timothy 2:5

4. Pray according to <u>God's will.</u> If you are using Scripture, you are on pretty safe ground.   Matthew 6:10

5. Don't be afraid to pray out loud. Jesus said to "<u>speak</u>" to the mountain (or problem) that you are addressing. Jesus healed people by speaking. God created the world through speaking. Words have power.
   Matthew 17:20   Genesis 1:3   Proverbs 18:21

6. Be <u>persistent</u> in prayer. Some mountains take longer to move!   Matthew 7:7   Matthew 17:20   Luke 18:1

7. Have someone you trust pray the same thing for you. That is called "<u>agreement</u>".   Matthew 18:20

8. Remember that <u>God loves you</u> and wants to answer you.   Hebrews 11:6

Distortions and Prayer

I don't want to overcomplicate prayer by giving you a lot of information. Like the Nike commercial says, "Just Do It!". There are prayers in the Bible you can use such as Matthew 6:9-13 or Ephesians 3:14-21. You can pray a Scripture over a person or a problem that concerns you. But most of the time you may want to just talk to God.

So, here is where distortions come in again. Often times, people have trouble praying. There are probably a lot of reasons why that is so. Many people worry that they aren't doing it right. I am convinced God is more interested in our attitude rather than in our skill. I believe He wants us to talk to Him and doesn't mind how good we are at it.

Think about how easy it was to talk to your dad/mom/authority figures growing up. Did they listen? Did they value what you thought? Were they able to enjoy you as a unique person or did they need you to be a certain way? Problems with communication, vulnerability, acceptance, and self esteem spill over into how comfortable we are in approaching God to pray.

God is interested in you as a person. He wants you to talk about your dreams, disappointments, frustrations, questions, and anger. He is big enough to handle it. If you ever read the Book of Psalms or Job you will see that His close friends (like David and Job) could rant and God did not shut them down.

One other idea about prayer. Often times, people tell me things they sense from God while they are praying. They sense criticism and that they are not trying hard enough. If you look back at the diagram about grace and religion (on page 31), you will see that those impressions are probably SELF judgments that aren't from God. When God corrects us, He will be gentle and specific unless we are deliberately rebelling against Him (Psalm 85:8-10).

Keys to Spiritual Health and Power

As long as you are yielded to God and trying to follow Him, He will continue to help you to grow (Philippians 1:6). It has taken me many years as a Christian to learn some of these things. Putting all this information in one place is designed to make your journey smoother.

The following sections describe various spiritual disciplines. These are not new commandments or religious rules to follow. These practices strengthen your spirit and ability to participate with God in your sphere of influence. If these are new to you, you want to make your priorities: 1) establish a daily time of reading your Bible and 2) establish a daily time of prayer and meditation. You have to take time to feed your spirit if you want to grow!

God's Word Is Living

The word of God is compared to bread (Matthew 4:4). Feeding on His word quickens our spirits just like eating bread nourishes our bodies. Drinking in God's word cleanses our system from toxic thinking and attitudes (John 17:17, Ephesians 5:26-27). The Bible calls this process "renewing" our minds (Romans 12:2).

Saturating our minds in God's word equips us to counter the criticism of others and the lies we have come to believe about ourselves and God (Ephesians 4:23-25). Declaring God's word moves us out of the box of our own limits and moves us into the supernatural purposes and power of God. When we know the Bible, God can use His word to speak to us when we need direction or comfort (Psalm 119:130, Isaiah 30:21).

An interesting point about the power of God's word is that even Jesus quoted Scripture. When the devil tried to create doubt in Jesus about His identity, the Father's love for Him, and the necessity of the Cross, Jesus protected Himself with Scripture (Luke 4:1-13). If Jesus used Scripture to fight darkness, then it is going to be important for us to know how to do the same (Psalm 119:11).

"I will give you the keys of the kingdom of heaven..."

Jesus

Matthew 16:19

Personal Devotions

The Lord will lead you as you start to incorporate spiritual disciplines into your life. Ordinarily, the best way to make change is to start small and be consistent. For most people, cultivating a lifestyle of worship to deepen their connection with the Lord starts with establishing a daily prayer and devotional time in the Bible.

- Ten minutes every day is generally more effective than long sessions of Bible reading a few times per week. You can build other components into your life when you are successful with one or two.

- Consistency builds relationship. Talk to God throughout the day and listen for His answers. The spiritual strength that God builds into you through your private time with Him will give you a foundation that is not easily shaken when the storms of life hit. God prepared David to slay Goliath during the years he watched sheep and wrote songs to God (known as "The Psalms").

As you get to know God better and learn what His word says, then your faith will grow. You will learn to sense His presence and "hear" His voice. You will have more wisdom in how to pray. You will begin to see God's hand in your daily life and recognize answers to prayer. You will learn to abide in His Spirit and live life more out of the supernatural realm with God (which He offers to all His children).

Questions to Consider

1. What is a new idea to you from this section?

2. What are your thoughts on the role of the Bible and prayer in spiritual growth?

3. What do you think could interfere with you having consistent time with God to read the Bible?

4. What distortions might be operating in your approach to prayer?

5. What is helpful to you from this section?

YouTube Videos:
Dr. Toni Cooper   "How To Pray With Power"
                         "Does Prayer Really Work? Why and How"
                         "How To Use The Keys To The Kingdom"
                         "Who's In Charge?"

Biblical Meditation

We are encouraged to meditate on God's word so that it gets deep into the core of our being (Joshua 1:8, Psalm 119:15, Colossians 3:16). God's word gives us wisdom (Psalm 119:130, Psalm 19:7). We need that wisdom and discernment to know how to pray, what to declare, and how to recognize His leading. His truth helps us correct deeply held distortions. Biblical meditation is a powerful tool that helps us comprehend the supernatural realm of God.

Various religions and even occult groups use meditation. Biblical meditation is distinctive in that we are instructed to *fill* (as opposed to *empty*) our minds. We can feed our spirits by filling our minds with God's word (Joshua 1:8, Psalm 19:14, Psalm 119:11). Another form of Biblical meditation is focusing on God's presence or one of the attributes of God (Psalm 63:6). Madame Jean Guyon and Brother Lawrence have written works that describe simple yet powerful ways to meditate. (I will guide you through a different meditation strategy later in the book.)

Simply put, meditation is pondering a verse of Scripture slowly, over and over, so that we draw out the fullness of its meaning. You can look up the meaning of key words. You can repeat the verse and emphasize a different word each time you read it. Each repetition, using a new emphasis, reveals a different shade of meaning. (You can observe this if you've ever seen an actor rehearsing their lines. They try out different ways to say the line and emphasize a different word each time.)

I've heard meditation compared to the way a person chews gum to draw out the flavor. If you think about it, we chew our food, rather than devour it, in order to enjoy the flavor and to digest it more thoroughly. In the same way, we can take time to meditate on God's word, rather than rushing through it, to draw out the richness. Meditation allows for deeper processing and nourishing of our spirits. Our lives are transformed as we allow God's word to penetrate our hearts and renew our minds (Hebrews 4:12, Romans 12:2).

We tend to think of meditation as something we do quietly. However, we can meditate out loud. Then, we drink in the richness of God's word as we declare the power of God's truth over our lives.

We can add another dimension to meditation by using an image or song to plant a truth deep into our spirits. For example, during a lengthy recovery from an injury, I meditated on the verse "your youth is renewed like the eagle" (Psalm 103:5). I printed that verse on a picture of a soaring eagle and posted it in a prominent place in my home. I was reminded constantly, and could meditate on and declare the verse, that God was restoring me. That picture and Scripture helped me stay spiritually and mentally strong during a long, discouraging process.

Earlier, we looked at pictures of God's loving attention to us (page 43). I have meditated on some of those pictures to help me "see" and experience God more clearly. You can ask God for a Bible verse to help you build your faith and spirit in an area of personal need. As we digest truth, distortions lose their hold in our thinking.

To clarify, we can strengthen our connection to God through prayer (talking to God) and reading the Bible (listening to God's thoughts). To get more of God's truth into our thinking, Biblical meditation is a powerful tool that assists in our transformation and the strengthening of the spirit. We can meditate on the presence of God (abiding) or we can meditate on the word of God.

For God will never give you

the spirit of fear,

but the Holy Spirit who gives you

mighty power, love, and self control.

2 Timothy 1:7

TPT

Power in Biblical Meditation

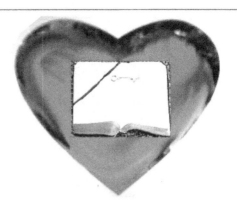

- Move God's living word from our heads to our hearts.

    Hebrews. 4:12

    Psalm 119:10-11

    Psalm 40:6-8

- Encounter God in a way that transforms our minds, quickens our spirit, and deepens personal revelation of truth as His Spirit touches ours through His Word.

    Ps. 119:18   Ps. 119:130   Romans 12:2   Ps. 19:7-8

- God reveals Himself and His secrets ~ satisfies and creates hunger.

    John 5:39   Ps. 63:5-8   Ps. 119:130   Ps. 25:4-15

- That well of deposits transforms us and increases conviction of truth, spiritual discernment, and emotional stability. Our spirit can draw from that well to encourage ourselves, help others, and pray with power.

    2 Tim. 3:16-17   Ps. 1:2-3   John 15:7   Eph. 6:17-18

- Helps us boldly persevere and succeed in our true destiny/purpose.

    Joshua 1:8-9   Ps. 1:1-3   Rom. 15:4

- Releases healing.

    Psalm 107:20   Prov. 16:24   Prov. 4:20-22

> "But you shall receive power
>
> (ability, efficiency, and might)
>
> when the Holy Spirit has come upon you"
>
> Jesus   Acts 1:8a   (AMP)

Supernatural Power for Living

In a way it's just common sense that if we want a supernatural life then we need supernatural power! God has taken care of that need along with our salvation.

Jesus said it was necessary that He return to heaven so that He could send us the Holy Spirit (John 16:7). When we invite Jesus to be our Savior, it is our spirit that becomes alive (Ephesians 2:1, 5; Colossians 2:13; Ezekiel 36:26-27). The Spirit of Jesus (that is, the Holy Spirit) abiding in our spirits allows His resurrection life and power to flow through us (Romans 8:11, Romans 12:11).

Every person who has received Jesus as his or her Savior has the Holy Spirit in them (Ephesians 1:13, 2 Corinthians 5:5). But every believer makes a decision concerning how much of *themselves* they give to Jesus each day. We can choose to be full of ourselves or we can yield to be full of the Holy Spirit (John 3:30, Romans 12:1, Ephesians 5:18).

The Bible teaches that Jesus came to baptize us with the Holy Spirit and with fire (Matthew 3:11, Luke 3:16). His fire gives us courage and strength to fight life's battles. All we have to do is ask to be filled each day. God wants us to have the power we need to live every day filled with His love and fire.

I'm going to address another distortion here. God doesn't want to cancel out your personality. He created you as a unique human being. Rather, He offers to fill our spirit with His goodness so that the best in our personality (soul) is empowered by Him. His Holy Spirit helps us develop: "joy that overflows, peace that subdues, patience that endures, kindness on display, a life full of virtue, faith that prevails, gentleness of heart, and strength of spirit" (Galatians 5:22-23 TPT).

This concept of living out of our spiritual union with Christ is taught throughout the New Testament. That is the whole point of Jesus sending the Holy Spirit (John 14:16-18). Some passages call this union abiding (John 15:4-5), walking in the Spirit (Galatians 5:16), and being filled or aglow with the Spirit (Romans 12:11, Ephesians 5:18).

Many try to live the Christian life out of the soul (intellect, emotions, self will). Those are the *natural* parts of our personality. When we try to live the Christian life out of our souls, we maintain control of our personal lives. When we demand full control, we are unplugged from our source of power while trying to get supernatural results (John 4:23-24, John 3:6, John 15:4-5).

Just like Jesus relied on the leading of the Holy Spirit, so we can learn to "lean in" and allow Jesus to direct us through His Holy Spirit. Jesus taught that when we take His yoke, we find rest (Matthew 11:28-30). In Bible days, a yoke was worn around the neck of two animals while they plowed. That was a picture that everyone would have understood back then. Today, that means when we partner with Jesus, He is doing the "heavy lifting" as long as we are moving in sync with Him.

It is God's power through His Holy Spirit that transforms us. His power then infuses our prayers, cleanses our motives, and draws out the best in our personalities. He gives us courage and vision to make a difference in our sphere of influence. We begin to live and think beyond the limits of our soul.

All that being said, a supernatural lifestyle is a choice. Supernatural life is the not result of self discipline (although daily personal devotions will assist in the process). Self will or self discipline alone is human effort to get a polished self. What we produce in our own strength does not impress God (John 15:4-5).

A supernatural life is learning to lean into Jesus so closely that He lives through us (2 Corinthians 5:17). We are fully alive in Him and live out of our union with Him (Colossians 2:9-10).

Summary

God doesn't expect us to be perfect. However, He does desire for us to be truthful with Him, ourselves, and others (Psalm 51:6). There are steps we can take to advance from glory to glory. As we yield more of ourselves to God, we become increasingly free from distortions in the way we see Him. As we lean into Jesus, we have the power of the Holy Spirit to live out of *our* spirit and be less dominated by our soul or unhealthy physical appetites.

Questions to Consider

1. What is a new idea to you about God?

2. What did you learn about the Holy Spirit?

3. We need God's help to love and obey Him. That takes the power of His HOLY Spirit. If you like, you can ask Jesus right now to freshly baptize you in His love and in His Holy Spirit.

4. Each day you can ask God to cleanse you and then fill up your spirit. Ask Him to teach you how to lean into His Spirit all day long. Confess to God your sin throughout the day as you become aware of it. Then ask Him to refill you. God makes this simple for us.

Resources: YouTube videos "Aglow With The Spirit", "Harnessing The Power Of The Spirit", and "Strengthening Your Spirit"

In Spirit and in Truth

Jesus taught us about how to pray, approach the Father, love each other, and worship. In John 4:23-24, Jesus explains two qualities that God looks for in His followers. He wants our worship to come out of our spirits and to be based on truth.

I've been a Christian many years, but I haven't heard much teaching about these verses for some reason. They seem important to me! You can ask God to help you understand what He is saying for yourself (Psalm 119:18, Ephesians 1:17-18).

First, let's look at what it means to worship the Father in spirit. We saw how the Bible teaches that our spirits are dead until we receive Jesus as our Savior. At the time we make a conscious choice to give our lives to Jesus our spirits come to life! At that moment, we receive spiritual life and we become children of God (John 1:12). When our spirits are alive with the fullness of the living God within us, we also have unlimited access to God through Jesus (Hebrews 4:15-16). So, the first part of worshipping in spirit is we have to have a spirit that has been brought to life.

Worship from our spirit means that we don't *just* approach God from our brain, habit, or even our emotion. (That would be worshipping out of our souls.) The spirit connection is where we access God in the power of His presence (not from *our* habit of religion).

> God is spirit,
>
> and those who worship Him
>
> must worship in spirit and truth...
>
> for such people the Father seeks
>
> to be His worshipers.
>
> John 4:24, 23b   NASB

So, what does it mean to worship in truth? First of all, Jesus says He is the only way to the Father because He *is* the way, the truth and the life (John 14:6). Our access is not through our own good works or any other person (Ephesians 2:8-9, I Timothy 2:5, Hebrews 12:24). So to worship God in truth must mean that we recognize our access to God is through Jesus.

I think to worship in truth also means that God desires that His children approach Him as He truly is. (Don't we want our close friends to know us as we are - not as they think we should be?) We already know that God does not want to be misrepresented as a ruthless tyrant. He is not touched by robotic obedience or guilty striving. We don't approach God flippantly, either, if we are a true worshipper.

> Therefore I urge you, brethren, by the mercies of God,
>
> to present your bodies a living and holy sacrifice,
>
> acceptable to God,
>
> which is your spiritual service of worship.
>
> And do not be conformed to this world,
>
> but be transformed by the renewing of your mind,
>
> so that you may prove what the will of God is,
>
> that which is good and acceptable
>
> and perfect.
>
> Romans 12:1-2 NASB

Another aspect of this principle is that God desires truth in our innermost being (Psalm 51:6, Psalm 15:2, Psalm 139:23-24). That means we can be real with God about who we are. We can be honest with ourselves and with God about our motives and struggles. We don't have to pretend to be better than we are or use "holy" language when we talk to Him. What a relief!

Moving to the idea of worship, it is actually good for us to worship God. Human beings long for a connection to something greater than themselves. That's why all cultures devise some form of worship. In fact, people and cultures are defined by what they worship. If we are not worshipping God, we will worship an ideology, another person, the pursuit of pleasure, or ourselves. Maybe you remember the Bob Dylan song, "Gotta Serve Somebody"?

Putting the pieces together, it seems that the more accurately we see God, the more pleasing is our worship, and the deeper is our connection to Him. In turn, distortions in our view of God, ourselves, and others are corrected over time. That is the process of sanctification and the renewing of our minds (Romans 12:1-2).

We know will never see God perfectly while we are on earth. He desires that we get to know Him as He really is and worship Him as a mighty, loving God.

There are many avenues and creative ways to worship God in spirit and in truth (John 4:23-24). There are spiritual disciplines, which are forms of worship, that you can build into your lifestyle. These disciplines are like roots that go deep into your spirit strengthening your connection to God. Then, no matter what happens, your life is intertwined with God. Your supernatural connection to God (that is, your spirit union in Christ) becomes as real as any other relationship.

So, connecting these ideas with the chapter on experiential knowledge, we can have a relationship with God that goes beyond accumulating doctrine. (The worship of doctrine is more like a Pharisee.) I have listed some ideas on how to show your love to God through your own personal worship.

Creative Worship

There are different ways to express worship just like there are different ways to express love. Some different ways to worship God are through:

- Singing,
- Dancing,
- Reading the Bible,
- Playing an instrument,
- Writing a song about His love or power (Psalm 63:6-7),
- Painting a picture that declares His beauty or majesty,
- Creating flags or banners that declare His word,
- Writing a play about a blessing from God,
- Obeying Him, and
- Giving of time, money, or talent.

Psalms 100 and 149 are two of the many psalms that describe worship. We can worship God in quiet and reverence (Psalm 46:10). We can be loud and passionate with our praise (Psalm 150).

Although your particular expression of worship can be creative, the purpose of worship is to demonstrate your love for God. The Bible tells us that the way to enter God's presence is through thanksgiving and praise (Psalm 100:4). Church participation means more when we know why we are singing (or dancing) and what is happening at the spiritual level.

The Bible teaches that our obedience to God's principles is another form of worship (Romans 12:1-2). Next we will look at the role of obedience to grow in wisdom and spiritual understanding.

God's "Miracle Grow" Formula

When I was growing up, I was introduced to a product called "Miracle Grow". I put it on my house plants and they would grow and flower into lush, hearty plants. It provided just the right nutrients for that plant to blossom and thrive.

So, God knows what we need to blossom and thrive We draw closer to Jesus when we follow the plan for living that is outlined in God's word, the Bible. That is not a popular concept in this day and age. People want to do things their own way. But, if you want the fullness of God's blessings, you will choose to yield to His leading and principles for living. In fact, the Bible teaches that obedience is a form of worship (Romans 12:1-2).

He leads us in the path of life (Psalm 16:11). His is the safest path. It is a choice whether or not we follow. Again, we choose whether or not to cultivate that deep relationship with God as a lifestyle.

If we respond to God's blessings and word as a buffet, picking and choosing the parts we want to follow, then we place limits on our growth. As we get to know God, yielding to His gentle invitations to us, then we move from glory to glory into deeper and deeper levels of His supernatural promises, power, and wisdom. It is our choice each day.

"Be careful what you are hearing.

The measure of thought and study you give

to the truth you hear

will be the measure of virtue and

knowledge that comes back to you -

and more besides will be given to you who hear."

Jesus

Mark 4:24 (Amplified)

Mark 4:24

God's **Miracle Grow** Method

Yielded Life

Deeper **Longing** for God   **Deeper** Abiding

Increased **Evidence** of God's **Presence** and **Power**

The closer we lean into the Lord, the more we will want to obey Him. The more we spend time with Him in various forms of worship (prayer, casual conversation, Bible reading, resting in His presence, art, dance, etc.) then the closer we are knit to Him. We will understand Him and His word better.

This strength and clarity allows me, like Jesus, to bring the kingdom of heaven into my sphere of influence on earth (Matthew 6:10). I have the courage to confront obstacles and live an extraordinary life. I find it easier to break old patterns and break through into blessings for myself and others.

Questions to Consider

1. What is a new idea to you about God?

2. What does it mean to worship in spirit?

3. What do you think it means to worship in truth?

4. How do you personally find it most enjoyable to worship God?

5. How does obedience to God relate to transformation and spiritual power?

YouTube Videos:

Dr. Toni Cooper   "Transformation Through Worship"
                       "The Process of Transformation I and II"

Biblical Meditation Strategy

Here is a chance for us to pause and practice some of the key principles we have looked at together. Biblical meditation gives us the chance to incorporate the Bible, prayer, and abiding in a simple way.

I learned this "DICE" method and used it for many years to help me understand the Bible and clear up some distortions. (I don't know where I learned this approach to reading the Bible.) This method can be used for meditation or for personal Bible study.

DICE Method

D - Define Key Words

I - In Your Own Words

C - Cross Reference/Context

E - Emphasize different words while you read the verse out loud

Let's meditate on a verse. I have done the research for you so you can enjoy the treasures. I selected a verse from Isaiah that means a lot to me.

There are many study tools you can use to define the key words. There are free Bible apps that allow you to check what a word from the Bible means in the original languages. (Most of the Bible was written in Hebrew or Greek.) But it is fine to use a dictionary if that is easier for you.

Before you start, you might want to ask God to speak to you as you read and soak in His word. You can make this exercise a time to enter into God's presence.

> For thus the Lord GOD, the Holy One of Israel, has said,
> "In repentance and rest you will be saved,
> In quietness and trust is your strength." Isaiah 30:15a

1. <u>Define Key Words</u>:

Here are definitions from The Theological Wordbook of the Old Testament. The numbers in the parentheses are for the entry number and page where the word is defined. Again, you can also use a dictionary to consider the meaning of key words. Just read the definitions to see what "flavor" you get for that word.

Holy (#1990b, p787)   sacred, perfect, separate from human impurity, totally good and without evil, exalted on a throne

Repentance (#2340a, p910)   returning, withdrawal

Rest (#1323a, p562)   victory, wellbeing, wholeness

Quietness (#2453, p953)   calm, tranquil, undisturbed

Trust (#233b, p101-102)   confidence, freedom from striving

Strength (#310c, p148)   royal power, courage, might, triumph, inner strength, victory in warfare

2. <u>In your own words</u>, rewrite the verse, substituting definitions for the key words that seem meaningful *to you*. If you like, place your name in the verse somewhere like this is a note written to you from God. (In a way, it is a note from God to us.)

3. <u>Cross Reference</u>. Scriptures that address the same ideas help us get perspective and balance on a topic. Many Bibles (or apps) will give you cross references in the margins or notes. I chose some cross references here for you. Just "chew" on them as you read.

    <u>Zechariah 4:6b</u>

    "...Not by might nor by power,

    but by My Spirit" says the LORD of hosts.

    <u>Psalm 23:2b-3</u>

    He leads me beside quiet waters.

    He restores my soul;

    <u>Ephesians 2:8-9</u>

    For by grace you have been saved through faith; and that not of yourselves, it is the gift of God; not as a result of works, so that no one may boast.

4. <u>Emphasize different words</u>. Go back to Isaiah 30:15. Read it out loud a few times. Try putting the emphasis on different key words. See if it speaks to you in a different way when you shift the emphasis.

Now you have had some experience with Biblical meditation. Here are words you can pray over yourself based on the meditation from Isaiah 30:15.

Thank You, Lord, that as I rest in You, I find peace for my heart and mind. Thank You that You recharge me with Your goodness, confidence, and royal power for living. I don't have to strive for Your attention because You are always watching over me.

I confess my sin to You, Lord, of _____ and I ask You for forgiveness. Thank You that You forgive me and keep leading me to peace and victory. You fight my battles with me as the Lord of Hosts. Help me walk in Your peace today.

Questions to Consider

1. What did you learn about God's word from this lesson?

2. What benefits do you see for yourself by using Biblical meditation in your devotional time?

3. What would you say is the main thing you feel like God is teaching you right now about connecting to Him?

YouTube videos "How To Read The Bible And Understand It", "Winning Your Battle", and "A Prayer of Blessing"

Spiritual Health and Balance

Here are some bullet points that summarize how to have spiritual health in Jesus. This type of lifestyle, which helps you learn how to live out of your spirit, will help you be more balanced, unload distortions, develop spiritual power, and be a positive influence with (rather than be unduly influenced by) the people around you. God wants us to be whole.

Spiritual Health

- KNOW that you have made Jesus your source for your spiritual life.
    I John 5:11-13   Philippians 3:10

- Take time daily to PRAY and talk to God.

    Philippians 4:6   I Peter 5:7

- Take time to READ the Bible and listen to God.

    Psalm 46:10   II Timothy 3:16

- "BATHE" by confessing your sin to God each day.

    I John 1:6-10   Psalm 51:6-7

- Let others Christians help you. Be REAL with people you can trust.

    Eccl. 4:9-10   Proverbs 27:17

- Take care of your "TEMPLE" because you only get one. People need rest, physical activity, healthy food, and leisure to be balanced and whole.

    I Corinthians 3:16   I Thessalonians 5:23

- INVEST in the work of God and other people so He can multiply blessings to you.

    Acts 10:4   II Corinthians 9:6-7

- Learn how to grow in your faith with other maturing believers.

    I Cor. 12:1-31   Ephesians 4:11-16

The Role Of Healthy Connections

Psychologist Larry Crabb wrote that people are changed by the word of God, the Spirit of God, and the people of God. We are all social beings who are designed to need others. Fear or pride may cause us to avoid the connections we need to mature in Christ and enter fully into the supernatural lifestyle He offers us.

God intends for us to live in a "body" or community of faith (I Corinthians 12:4-27, Ephesians 4:11-16). The Bible explains that if the physical foot decides, "I've had enough", it will not survive separated from the body. It is dismembered. So, we will not thrive separated from meaningful connection to other believers who are actively seeking God.

The Bible teaches that every believer has spiritual gifts (I Corinthians 12:1-17, Ephesians 4:7-16, Romans 12:4-11). These can be natural talents you were born with that are energized by the Holy Spirit (like a gift of teaching). We need the gifts that other people bring to the body and they need ours. We learn to function in our gifts with other people of faith. Jesus taught His disciples how to use their gifts and we can read about that in the Gospels (Matthew, Mark, Luke, and John in the New Testament). The disciples taught people how to use their spiritual gifts in the Epistles (letters) they wrote to help new believers grow in their faith. When we are operating in our spiritual gifts we will feel fulfilled and energized

Besides spiritual gifts, other people have strength where we have weakness. Those differences can help us find balance. The input of truth and love from people who care about us helps us recognize our blind spots (or faulty thinking) that damage our faith, healthy confidence, and relationships.

On a personal note, I have a lot of tendencies toward introversion. When I was in graduate school, I became friends with a *very* outgoing and confident student who was in many of my classes. After being around him for several months, I realized I was becoming more friendly and outgoing myself. That friendship was a gift from God to help me find balance.

> Two are better than one
>
> because they have a good return
>
> for their labor.
>
> For if either of them falls,
>
> the one will lift up his companion.
>
> But woe to the one who falls
>
> when there is not another to lift him up.
>
> Ecclesiastes 4:9-10 NASB

If we are honest, we need to admit that human beings often minimize or excuse our faults (if we see them at all). We all need gentle doses of truth delivered with love. We can build relationships with other humble people who acknowledge their flaws and broken places. (These principles are the very reason that AA and other 12 Step groups are so successful.) We can *share* the journey into spiritual maturity. A healthy church or fellowship group is permeated with the truth, love, and humility of Jesus Christ (Psalm 85:8-10, Psalm 89:14, Isaiah 53:2, John 1:17).

We need a community of fellow believers (and a few good friends) who will gently tell us the truth and encourage us as we learn and grow. We need to be patient with ourselves and others in the process of transformation. Without compromising the truth of the Bible, we need to relate to each other with an attitude of humility and mercy (Galatians 6:1-4; Ephesians 4:15-16; Romans 12: 3, 16; I Peter 5:5-6; I Peter 4:8). Then, we enjoy the journey together.

A healthy spiritual community has healthy boundaries. People are not used as workhorses (or slaves) for the church's agenda. Sexual boundaries are not crossed with children, teens, or adults. Healthy churches don't bleed people financially or keep secrets when there is violence or abuse.

Please don't blame God for church dysfunction. People are messy inside and outside of church! Next, we will look at boundaries and protection.

Community

We are not designed to walk the Christian life alone. We need other positive believers around us who are strong enough to love us and celebrate our progress. We need people to encourage us and be patient with us when we are in a crisis.

Sometimes we need people to show us the love of God when our hearts are too heavy to feel it for ourselves. We need to seek out fellowship with other believers more than ever in those times (Romans 12:4-15, Hebrews 10:23-25). We don't need to be ashamed of our weaknesses. Use wisdom about whom you trust, but

- Talk to a friend,
- Find a prayer partner,
- Make an appointment with your pastor,
- Share a prayer request,
- Join a Bible study,
- Call a prayer line, and/or
- Find a church.

We need to move past pride or fear. Nearly everyone has been through their own hardships, failures, and losses. Nearly everyone has times where they have struggled in matters of faith. We need other people and they need us. The journey is more fun with company!

Protecting Yourself and Your Boundaries

I have found that people of faith often have terrible boundaries. They often have the distortion that God expects them to take care of everyone if they are a good Christian. Exhausting or neglecting ourselves (or our loved ones) is not healthy or Christian. Even Jesus took time to rest and delegated responsibility to His disciples. If Jesus needed rest and boundaries, then we do too!

Our boundaries can be too loose, too tight, or balanced. We all err in one direction or another. (If this is an interest for you, check out the book by Dr. Henry Cloud listed on the Resources page.) If you know where you tend to err, you can ask God to help you find balance. We need healthy connections to others that encourage our own balance. Excessive caretaking of others is not healthier than withdrawing from other people. We all need balance.

If you are gifted with compassion, you are not designed to carry all the burdens of others. We are told to carry those burdens to Jesus and leave them to Him (I Peter 5:7). Otherwise, we are likely to burn ourselves out *and* cross over from helping to enabling.

I find that even people who pray often don't know how to pray effectively about their relationships. Many do not pray for themselves at all! I see this as a boundary problem. We don't want to be a casualty on the battlefield of life because we failed to protect ourselves.

Although there is no substitute for healthy communication, sometimes problems do not seem to resolve in relationships. In those situations, we may need to turn completely to prayer (declaring truth) to see breakthrough. We may also need to adjust our boundaries and expectations. Few people seem to know how to make those adjustments.

Next, I want to share more principles on how to pray for yourself and your family, loved ones, community, etc. We will have suffering on earth, no matter how much we pray, but effective prayer can minimize some of the pitfalls. On the next few pages, we will look at aggressive prayer strategies using declaration and covenant principles.

> In the beginning was the Word, and the Word was with God, and the Word was God.
>
> John 1:1 NASB

Prayers of Declaration

We can underestimate the power of the spoken word. God *spoke* creation into existence (Genesis 1). One of the names for Jesus is "the Word" (John 1:1).

It is God's word, not our words or the power of positive thinking, that produces supernatural change (Hebrews 4:12, Isaiah 55:11). When we use our words to speak life and blessing (for ourselves and others) we allow God to move in the situation. When we speak negative, complaining, hopeless words to ourselves or others, we take a step back into the darkness (Proverbs 18:21). We need to take seriously the power of the words coming out of our mouths.

Sometimes, even our prayers are nothing more than complaining to God. I think it's okay to vent to God (Job and David did). But sometimes our prayers need to go beyond venting or requests.

We Carry Resurrection Power

Every believer carries the resurrection life and light of Jesus (Romans 8:9-11, John 1:4). When we speak His word, we release the life and light of God into human circumstances (Matthew 6:10, John 1:4, Romans 4:17, Proverbs 18:21, Genesis 1:2-3).

That's another reason why it's important to know God's word. We can't speak His truth if we don't know what the Bible says. We see answers to prayer and radical transformations when we speak His will - His word - into chaos on earth (Romans 4:17). Speaking God's word, over ourselves and others, produces all kinds of positive results in our lives. Some people call that spiritual warfare prayer.

Jesus tells us to speak to our mountain of difficulty (Matthew 17:20). We saw before that Jesus spoke to problems using God's word. The difference between us and Jesus (well, one of the differences) is that Jesus always knew God's will. If we use a Scripture, then we are praying God's will and not our own. People get into trouble when they insist on praying their own will. Then, we are crossing boundaries.

It is always safe to pray a Scripture for health, order, peace, safety, etc. over a situation. Those are God's will. Here is an example of how to do this. Suppose there is a lot of conflict with someone in your life. Perhaps you have tried to speak with this person and it didn't go well. You probably will need to forgive them in your own heart. (I don't like it when someone *tells* me that they forgave me if I didn't ask them to forgive me. You probably don't like it, either.) In private, you might pray out loud something like this:

"Thank you, Lord, for your order and peace over me and _____. You are the Prince of Peace. Lord, I invite You into this situation. You desire for us to know truth in our innermost being (Psalm 51:6). Thank You that you are flooding the eyes of our hearts with Your light (Ephesians 1:18) and that You guide us in the path of life (Psalm 16:11). I ask You to release Your love, truth, and healing over this situation. I ask You for wisdom. I bless _____ today and I give You permission to show me anything You want me to know about myself or my boundaries and expectations."

Declaring is more than a request. It is pronouncing God's word over a problem (in a positive way). If the Lord gives you a special verse to pray, then use that. He gives us wisdom in how to pray (Romans 8:26-27, James 1:5). Remember, we are praying His word for His will. When we pray our own will over a situation we may be crossing spiritual and emotional boundaries.

Sometimes we will have to adjust our boundaries or expectations in a relationship. It may be necessary to seek wise counsel about the problem. Make sure, when you do interact with the person, that you speak truth *and* grace. We don't always have to speak our minds.

Understanding Covenant Protection

Growing up, you may have made a pact with someone to be "Blood Brothers" or "Blood Sisters". The alliance was made by shedding blood.

In ancient civilizations, people established binding agreements or covenants by shedding the blood of animals in a solemn ritual. The covenant was a permanent commitment for the stronger family or individual to protect the weaker. In turn, the lesser tribe or person pledged their loyalty. In the Old Testament, God told the Israelites to put the blood of a sacrificial lamb over their doorposts when He was ready to judge their captors (Exodus 12:5-13, Hebrews 11:28). Every family whose door was marked by blood was protected from God's judgment. The Bible says that life is in the blood (Leviticus 17:11) and there is no forgiveness of sin without the shedding of blood (Hebrews 9:22).

Our salvation, or covenant with God, was divinely provided by the shedding of Jesus' blood (Romans 5:9, Colossians 1:20). That's one reason Jesus is called "the Lamb of God" (John 1:29, Revelation 5:12). When you have given your life to Jesus, you have entered into His covenant. At the Last Supper, as Jesus distributed the wine and bread, He told His disciples "for this is My blood of the covenant, which is poured out for many for forgiveness of sins" (Matthew 26:28).

The blood of Jesus continues to be the protection and deliverance for our personal lives and loved ones (Hebrews 12:24). One way to apply the blood now is by celebrating communion. You can also ask Jesus to cover your day, health, finances, travel, children, spouse, etc. with His shed blood. (I do this for myself and my grown daughter every morning.) When you pray that spiritual covering you are applying the blood just like the Israelites did. You are inviting God to cleanse and protect you according to the New Covenant.

If that seems too extreme for you, there are other ways to pray for protection. The most well known prayer is "The Lord's Prayer" that Jesus taught as one guide for us. You can find it in Matthew 6:9-13.

There is another passage in Ephesians called "The Armor of God". (The passage is printed below.) When my daughter was little, we would pray this together in the morning. We made up motions for each part of the armor as we put it on in prayer.

As you learn to exercise your spiritual authority in God you will have greater peace. You can understand better when it's time to set limits in situations that would needlessly disturb your wellbeing. You can pray and declare God's Word for protection, maintenance, and repair of relationships.

> Therefore, take up the full armor of God,
>
> so that you will be able to resist in the evil day,
>
> and having done everything, to stand firm.
>
> Stand firm, therefore,
>
> HAVING GIRDED YOUR LOINS WITH TRUTH, and
>
> HAVING PUT ON THE BREASTPLATE OF RIGHTEOUSNESS,
>
> and having shod YOUR FEET
>
> WITH THE PREPARATION OF THE GOSPEL OF PEACE;
>
> in addition to all, taking up the shield of faith
>
> with which you will be able to extinguish all the flaming arrows
>
> of the evil one.
>
> And take THE HELMET OF SALVATION,
>
> and the sword of the Spirit,
>
> which is the word of God.
>
> Ephesians 6:13-17 NASB

Questions to Consider

1. What is a new idea to you about God?

2. How can a person pray with power according to the Bible?

3. What is the difference between prayer and declaration?

4. What thoughts do you have about your boundaries?

5. What is one thing you would like to do to improve your connections to other people who follow Jesus?

YouTube Videos:
Dr. Toni Cooper   "Healthy Personal Boundaries"
                           "The Lost Teaching"
                           "Harnessing The Power Of The Spirit"
                           "Understanding Yourself And Others"

A Lifestyle of Transforming Faith

Here are some principles we have examined on how to live a transformed life. This life is characterized by a person who is positive, free, balanced, and demonstrates the fruit of the Holy Spirit (Galatians 5:22-23). Mark "True" for each faith principle that you already practice.

QUIZ: Transforming Faith

___1. I consistently read the Bible for myself (Psalm 40:7-8, Acts 17:11, II Timothy 2:15).

___2. I spend quiet time in prayer waiting for God to commune with and speak to me (Psalm 46:10; Psalm 85:8-10; John 10: 3, 27).

___3. I pray for myself and others regularly (I Peter 5:7, Matthew 7:7-11, I Timothy 2:1-2).

___4. I consistently obey what I know is right (John 14:21, Psalm 25:14).

___5. I spend time with other believers who help me learn and grow in my faith (Hebrews 10:24-25, Proverbs 27:17).

___6. I lean into Jesus each day for my direction and strength (John 15:4-5, Colossians 3:1).

___7. I am persistent in my faith (Hebrews 12:1-3, Galatians 6:9-10).

___8. I am humble but not weak. I yield to God's leading and I interact with others, especially leaders, in a respectful way (I Peter 5:5-6, Matthew 5:5).

___9. I devote time to helping others (James 1:27, James 2:14-17).

___10. I plan for time to worship God with others each week (Hebrews 10:24-25, Isaiah 58:13-14).

___11. I ask for prayer from others who can help me grow in my faith and spiritual gifts (Ephesians 3:14-21, Romans 1:9-12).

___12. I watch the words that come out of my mouth (II Timothy 2:16, James 1:26).

___13. I allow the Holy Spirit to search my heart and motives (Psalm 139:23-24, Hebrews 4:12, Psalm 51:6).

___14. I give a portion of my income to further God's kingdom on earth (2 Corinthians 9:6-7, Romans 12:13).

___15. I fast as God directs me (and as my doctor permits) (Isaiah 58:6).

For we come to God in faith

knowing that he is real

and that he rewards the faith

of those who passionately seek him.

Hebrews 11:6b TPT

Moving Past Our Comfort Zone

God still rewards those who diligently seek Him as a lifestyle (Jeremiah 29:11-13, Hebrews 11:6). A supernatural life is marked by devotion to Jesus and obedience that moves us beyond our comfort zone. We don't earn the blessings and favor of God, but there are ways that we can position ourselves to experience a greater measure of the supernatural life of God each day. We have looked at simple ways believers can develop transforming faith.

There are many accounts in Scripture of people who took radical steps to encounter Jesus. They were determined to move past the mundane and into the flow of supernatural life.

Zacchaeus climbed a tree to get a glimpse of Jesus in the crowd (Luke 19:1-10). He didn't care about his dignity or reputation. Jesus rewarded his determination. That day, the crowd got a *glimpse* of Jesus but Zacchaeus received a *visit* for his entire household.

Luke 8:43-48 records the testimony of a woman who had some sort of hemorrhage for twelve years. She had spent everything she had on medical treatments without any improvement. Because her illness involved blood, she was considered unclean so she was a social outcast on top of the medical problem. She was taking a big chance by pressing through the crowd and daring to touch Jesus. But the sincerity of her faith and determination was greeted by Jesus with tenderness, healing, and a public blessing.

In Mark 2:1-12, there is another healing recorded about people determined to see Jesus. The crowd was so thick around a home where Jesus was staying that four men dug a hole in the roof so that they could lower their paralyzed friend into the gathering. Recognizing their faith, Jesus forgave the paralyzed man's sins and healed his body.

Faith moves us to action for ourselves and other people. There is suffering on earth, but faith helps us to be proactive in situations that are bad for us or our loved ones. God gives us courage to keep going and be a person who carries life to others.

The Thrill of Letting Go

There is a part in most of us that finds it thrilling to let go. Some people like roller coasters. For others, it is the pleasure of a motorcycle ride or an adventure movie. Many look for a release from the slavery of self and stress.

Jesus said to truly find our lives, we have to lose them (Luke 9:24). In other words, the greatest joy in life is in losing ourselves in Him. When we build our trust in Jesus and release ourselves fully to Him, we enter a realm that deepens our connection. We experience more of His love and power. In a new way, we carry life into our sphere of influence. We find purpose that transcends our limited earthly focus. There is an excitement as we venture into the supernatural with the One who loves us and cares for us the most. We are designed to fly with Him like eagles (Exodus 19:4, Isaiah 40:31). We can never really be fulfilled living in the earth-bound prison of the self.

Jesus gives us His power to worship, love, obey, and live boldly through His indwelling Holy Spirit (Romans 8:11, Ephesians 5:18). Yielding to Jesus is, in essence, living out of our spirit instead of our intellect or emotion. Our confidence, relationships, and circumstances are important but can't rule us as they once did. We can discipline ourselves to achieve our goals. We can pray with power.

We know that our salvation is paid for by Jesus. Deep transformation and spiritual experience come from our own personal investment. The emphasis we place on opportunities for growth with likeminded people is our decision.

So, I encourage you to continue to find your life in Him. Set aside time to bask in His presence. Let Him (and others) gently correct your distortions. Follow Him into the new opportunities and experiences that are on His path of life for you (Psalm 16:11). Build kingdom relationships. Identify and develop your spiritual gifts. Keep seeking His wisdom for your daily life (James 1:5). Learn to exercise your spiritual authority in Jesus to build God's kingdom. There is no better way to find joy and purpose in life.

<u>Questions To Consider</u>

1. What has God been speaking to you about in these lessons?

2. What baggage do you think you have unloaded so far? (Remember, growth is a process and a lifestyle.)

3. What have you learned about how you can grow?

4. How would you describe your relationship to Jesus right now?

5. What would you like to do in order to deepen your relationship with the Lord and be able to mature and grow? Is there a way you want to build God's kingdom?

6. If you like, review the prayers on pages 44-49. Is there a prayer you want to use *now* to release a distortion?

<u>Thank you</u> for reading this book. If this helped you, I would love to hear your feedback. You can send me a message through Facebook (Dr. Toni Cooper) or Instagram (tonicooper777).

Resources And References

Arnott, John. (1997). <u>The Importance of Forgiveness</u>. Ventura, California: Renew Books.

Browne, J. (1972). Doctor My Eyes. On <u>Jackson Browne</u>. New York: Asylum Records.

Chavda, Mahesh. (1998). <u>The Hidden Power of Prayer and Fasting</u>. Shippensburg, Pennsylvania: Destiny Image Publishers, Inc.

Cloud, H. & Townsend, J. (1992). <u>Boundaries: When to Say Yes. How To Say No</u>. Grand Rapids, Michigan: Zondervan.

Cooper, T. (2019). <u>Breaking Through To Blessing: Keys To Unlock The Supernatural Blessings of God</u>. Available on Amazon.

Cooper, T. (2019). <u>Sheep Hear His Voice</u>. Available on Amazon.

Crabb, L. (1992). <u>Inside Out</u>. Colorado Springs: NavPress.

Dylan, R. (1979). Gotta Serve Somebody. On <u>Slow Train Coming</u>. New York: Columbia Records.

Foster, R. L. & Smith, J. B. (Eds.). (1993). <u>Devotional Classics</u>. New York: Renovare´, Inc.

Guyon, J. (1975). <u>Experiencing the Depths of Jesus Christ</u>. Jacksonville, Florida: SeedSowers Publishing. (First published in 1685 under the title "The Short and Easy Method of Prayer".)

Harris, R.L., Archer, G.L., Jr., & Waltke, B.K. (1980). <u>Theological Wordbook of the Old Testament</u>. Chicago: Moody Bible Institute.

Keller, W. P. (1970). <u>A Shepherd Looks at Psalm 23</u>. Grand Rapids, Michigan: Zondervan.

Lawrence, Brother. (1977). <u>The Practice of the Presence of God</u>. Translated by John J. Delaney. New York: Doubleday Publishing. (First published in 1691.)

Lewis, C. S. (1950). <u>The Lion, the Witch and the Wardrobe</u>. New York: HarperCollins Publishers.

Maloney, J. (2011). <u>The Dancing Hand of God</u> (Volume 1). Bloomington, Indiana: WestBow Press.

Rizzuto, A. M. (1979). <u>Birth of the Living God</u>. Chicago: The University of Chicago Press.

Seamands, D. (1981). <u>Healing For Damaged Emotions</u>. Colorado Springs: David C Cook.

YouTube Videos

Inspiration to help you become "Fully Alive"

VIDEOS
Dr. Toni Cooper

Coping Skills

* Basics
  - "Improve Your Coping Skills"
  - "Your Style of Coping"
  - "Reducing Perfectionism"
  - "Procrastination"
* Stress — "Strategies For Stress Management"
* Relaxation — "Relaxation With Imagery"
* Boundaries & Relationships
  - "Healthy Personal Boundaries"
  - "Relationship Addiction"
  - "Expectations in Committed Relationships"
  - "Understanding Yourself & Others"
* Self Confidence — "Building Self Confidence"
* Grief — "Grief, Loss, and Depression"

Coping Tools

* Dream Interpretation — "Understanding Your Dreams"
* Using a Journal
* Setting Goals
* Positive Affirmations — "Psychological Strategies For Change"
* Coaching Statements
* "I" sentences
* Obsessive Thinking — "Obsessive Thoughts"

Understanding Personality

1 – Insights Into HABITS, Triggers, and Problem Behavior
2 – Understanding Personality NEEDS
3 – Psychological Strategies For CHANGE
4 – Strengthening Your SPIRIT

PLAYLISTS

Prayers (26 videos)
Spiritual Freedom, Peace, and Effective Prayer

- Life Without Baggage
- Blessings For Wholeness
- Does Prayer Work? Why and How
- Are You Trapped In A Vow?
- Restoring Identity, Dignity, And Destiny
- Blessings For Peace And Wisdom
* A Prayer To Heal From Trauma
* A Prayer For Breakthrough
* A Prayer For Mending
* How to Pray With Power
* How To Ask God For Forgiveness
* How To FINALLY Forgive

Inspiration (45 videos)
Building Your Faith and Drawing Closer to God

- Great Expectations
- How to Hear the Gentle Voice of God
- The Gift of Peace
- Aglow with the Spirit
- Who Do You Follow?
* Toxic Guilt and Shame
* Law vs. Grace
* Eyes That See
* How To Read the Bible and Understand It

The Kingdom Of God (18 videos)
Developing Mature Faith and Advancing God's Kingdom

* Harnessing the POWER of the Spirit
* How to Use The Keys to the Kingdom
* A Prayer for Our Nation
* Winning Your Battle
* The Process of Transformation
* Strengthening Your Spirit
* Basics for Breakthrough
* The Lost Teaching

Follow me on social media!
Visit my website to find out about speaking engagements.

CREATED to be FULLY alive

Facebook — Dr. Toni Cooper
YouTube — Dr. Toni Cooper
Instagram — tonicooper777

Books on Amazon and Kindle

www.drtonicooper.com

Associated Works

Available on Amazon

Many people try to release baggage from the stresses of life but still feel stuck. The Bible illuminates how to recognize the hidden hooks to lingering baggage. This workbook will help you to recognize known and unknown sources of baggage, release them through guided prayer, and rebuild your life with the principles of Scripture.

Thirty thoughtful passages for personal inspiration. Each day includes selected Bible verses, an explanation of the verses, a color illustration, and simple questions to help you deepen your connection to God. This book is full of positive encouragement for anyone who is struggling as well as simple strategies to build your faith.

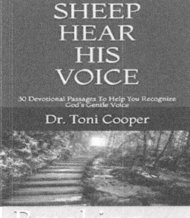

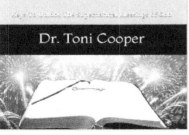

This Bible study examines the lessons Jesus taught His followers about how to release unusual blessings from God. Topics include building a confident faith, strength during difficulty, removing distortions about God, praying with power, and strategies that accelerate spiritual progress.

Made in the USA
Las Vegas, NV
19 November 2021